REMARKS

ON THE USES OF THE

DEFINITIVE ARTICLE

IN THE

GREEK TEXT OF THE NEW TESTAMENT,

Containing many New Proofs

OF THE

DIVINITY OF CHRIST,

From Passages which are wrongly translated
in the

COMMON ENGLISH VERSION.

BY GRANVILLE SHARP.

To which is added

AN APPENDIX,

Containing

1. A TABLE OF EVIDENCES OF CHRIST'S DIVINITY,
By Dr. Whitby.

2. A PLAIN ARGUMENT FROM THE GOSPEL HISTORY FOR THE DIVINITY OF CHRIST,
By the former learned Editor.

3. EXTRACTS FROM SELECTED REVIEWS.

Edited by
WILLIAM DAVID MCBRAYER

THE ORIGINAL WORD, INC.
ATLANTA 1995

To the glory of God

ISBN 0-9626544-4-2

Library of Congress Catalog Card Number 94-66339

Published by The Original Word Publishers
P.O. Box 799, Roswell, GA, 30077. USA.

The Original Word® and The Original Word® logo are registered trademarks of The Original Word Ministries, Inc.

CONTENTS.

RULE I.

When two personal nouns of the same case are connected by the copulative και, if the former has the definitive article, and the latter has not, they both relate to the same person

. . . . page 8

EXAMPLES.*

1. Ὁ Θεος και πατηρ του κυριου ἡμων 9
2. Τῳ Θεῳ και πατρι 13
3. Εν τη βασιλεια του Χπιστου και Θεου 42
4. Κατα την χαριν του Θεου ἡμων και κυριου Ιησου Χριστου, ... 45
5. Ενωπιον του Θεου και κυριου Ιησου Χριστου 48
6. Επιφανειαν της δοξης του μεγαλου Θεου και Σωτηρος ἡμων Ιησου Χριστου 35, 55
7. Εν δικαιοσυνη του Θεου ἡμων και Σωτηρος ἡμων Ιησου Χριστου 34, 56
8. Και τον μονον δεσποτην Θεον και κυριον ἡμων Ιησουν Χριστον αρνουμενοι 57

* [Ed. note: KJV translations of these examples appear on the next page. For reference, example 1- 2 Corinthians 1:3; example 2- James 1:27; example 3- Ephesians 5:5; example 4- 2 Thessalonians 4:12; example 5- 1 Timothy 5:21; example 6- Titus 2:13; example 7- 2 Peter 1:1; example 8- Jude 1:4]

(4)

Common Version.

1. The God and Father of our Lord.
2. To God, even the Father.

Corrected Version.   *Common Version.*

Corrected Version.	*Common Version.*
3. In the kingdom of Christ, even of God	In the kingdom of Christ, and of God.
4. According to the grace of Jesus Christ, our God and Lord.	According to the grace of our God, and the Lord Jesus Christ.
5. Before Jesus Christ, the God and Lord; *or*, our God and Lord: *for, the definite article has sometime the power of a passive* [*sic*: possessive] *pronoun.*	Before God, and the Lord Jesus Christ.
6. The glorious appearing of our great God and Saviour Jesus Christ.	The glorious appearing of the great God, and our Saviour Jesus Christ.
7. Through the righteousness of Jesus Christ, our God and Saviour.	Through the righteousness of God, and our Saviour Jesus Christ.
8. And denying our only Master, God, and Lord, Jesus Christ.	And denying the only Lord God, and our Lord Jesus Christ.

RULE II.

If both nouns have the article, but not the copulative, they relate to the same person . . . . page 14

RULE III.

If the first has the article, and the second has not, and there is no copulative, they relate also to the same person . . .19

RULE IV.

If the nouns are not personal, they relate to different things or qualities 21

RULE V.

If personal nouns, of the same case, are connected by the copulative, and the first has not the article, they relate to different persons 23

RULE VI.

If they are connected by the copulative, and both have the article, they relate also to different persons 25

A

LETTER

TO THE

Rev. Mr -----------,

CONCERNING THE USES OF THE GREEK ARTICLE

ὁ   IN THE NEW TESTAMENT.

Old Jewry, London, 10th June, 1778.

Dear Sir,

WHEN I look upon the date of your last obliging letter, I am much ashamed that I have so long neglected to acknowledge the receipt of it. The truth is, I began a letter a few days afterwards; but, recollecting that I had written on the same subject (viz. the use of the Greek article ὁ and copulative καὶ) to a very learned friend, at a great distance in the country, I was willing to wait for his answer, lest it should oblige me to make any alterations in my rules; and so, indeed, it has proved; for, he objected to my first rule, (as it was then stated,) and has cited several exceptions to it, which he thought sufficient to set it entirely aside: but this, I am convinced, is going too far, and would be an injury to truth. The use, therefore, which I have made of my friend's objections, has been, to correct my rule, and add to it such limitations as might include the several exceptions cited by my learned friend, as well as others that are similar to them.

The waiting for my friend's answer, and the necessary corrections in consequence of it, together with a variety of other engagements, have prevented me from complying with your request so soon as I could have wished; but I shall now submit to your consideration and candor the rules in question, and beg that you will be pleased to favor me with whatever example may occur in the course of your reading, either as exceptions to invalidate the *first rule*, or as proofs to establish and confirm it. The reason of my recommending the first rule more particularly to your attention, is, because it is of much more consequence than any of the rest, as it will enable us (if the truth of it be admitted) to correct the translation of several important texts in the present English version of the New Testament, in favor of a fundamental article of our church, which has, of late, been much opposed and traduced; I mean the belief that our Lord Jesus Christ is truly God.

RULE I.

When the copulative και *connects two nouns of the same case, [viz. nouns (either substantive or adjective, or participles) of personal description respecting office, dignity, affinity, or connection, and attributes, properties, or qualities, good or ill,] if the article* ὁ, *or any of its cases, precedes the first of the said nouns or participles, and is not repeated before the second noun or participle, the latter always relates to the same person that is expressed or described by the first noun or participle:* i.e. it denotes a farther description of the first-named person; as, —

[Ed. note: an interlinear has been added to Sharp's original Greek text to assist the reader; underlining has been added to replace the upper case letters used by Sharp for emphasis.]

Mat. 12:22.

καὶ	ἐθεράπευσεν	αὐτόν,		ὥστε	τὸν	τυφλὸν
and	he healed	him,		so that	the	blind

καὶ	κωφὸν	καὶ	λαλεῖν		καὶ	βλέπειν.
and	dumb	and	to speak		and	to see.

And, again, 2 Cor. 1:3.

Εὐλογητὸς	ὁ	Θεὸς	καὶ	Πατὴρ	τοῦ
Blessed	the	God	and	Father	of the

Κυρίου	ἡμῶν	Ἰησοῦ	Χριστοῦ,	ὁ
Lord	of us	Jesus	Christ	the

Πατὴρ	τῶν	οἰκτιρμῶν	καὶ	Θεὸς	πάσης
Father	of the	compassions	and	God	of all

παρακλήσεως.
comfort

This last sentence contains two examples of the first rule. See also in 2 Cor. 11:31,

ὁ	Θεὸς	καὶ	Πατὴρ	τοῦ	Κυρίου
the	God	and	Father	of the	Lord

ἡμῶν	Ἰησοῦ	Χριστοῦ	οἶδεν,	
of us	Jesus	Christ	knows,	etc.

Also in Eph. 6:21,

Τυχικὸς	ὁ	ἀγαπητὸς	ἀδελφὸς	καὶ
Tychicus	the	beloved	brother	and

(10)

πιστος	διακονος	εν	Κυριω.
faithful	minister	in	Lord.

Also in Heb. 3:1,

Κατανοησατε	τον	αποστολον	και	αρχιερεα
Consider	the	apostle	and	high priest

της	ὁμολογιας	ἡμων	Ιησουν	Χριστον,	
of the	confession	of us	Jesus	Christ,	etc.

See also in 2 Pet. 2:20,

εν	επιγνωσει	του	Κυριου	και	Σωτηρος
In (by)	a full knowledge	of the	Lord	and	Saviour

Ιησου	Χριστου	
Jesus	Christ,	etc.

And again, in 2 Pet. 3:2,

και	της	των	αποστολων	ἡμων	εντολης,
and	the	of the	apostles	of you	command

του	Κυριου	και	Σωτηρος.
of the	Lord	and	Saviour,

And again, in 2 Pet. 3:18,

Αυξανετε	δε εν	χαριτι	και	γνωσει
grow ye	But in	grace	and	knowledge

του	Κυριου	ἡμων	και	Σωτηρος	Ιησου
of the	Lord	of us	and	Saviour	Jesus

(11)

Χριστου.	αυτω	ἡ	δοξα	και	νυν	και
Christ.	To him	the	glory	and	now	and

εις	ἡμεραν	αιωνος,	αμην.
unto	a day	of age	amen.

Also in Philippians, 4:20,

Τῳ	δε	Θεῳ	και	Πατρι	ἡμων	ἡ
to the	Now	God	and	Father	of us	the

δοξα	
glory,	etc.

In Rev. 16:15,

μακαριος	ὁ	γρηγορων	και	τηρων	τα
blessed	the [one]	watching	and	keeping	the

ἱματια	αὐτου,	ἱνα	μη	γυμνος
garments	of him,	in order that	not	naked

περιπατη	
he walk,	etc.

And in Col. 2:2, [Col. 2:2,3]

εις	επιγνωσιν	του	μυστηριου	του	Θεου
for	full knowledge	of the	mystery	of the	God

και	Πατρος	και	του	Χριστου*,	εν	ὡ
and	Father	and	of the	Christ	in	whom

* The distinction of persons mentioned in this sentence is preserved by the insertion of the article του before Χριστου, which had been omitted before Πατρος.

(12)

εισι	παντες	ὁι [sic - οἱ]	θησαυροι	της	σοφιας
are	all	the	treasures	of the	wisdom, etc.

And in 1 Thes. 3:11,

Αυτος	δε	ὁ	Θεος	και	Πατηρ
[Him] self	Now	the	God	and	Father

ἡμων	και	ὁ	Κυριος	ἡμων	Ιησους
of us	and	the	Lord	of us	Jesus

Χριστος,	κατευθυναι	την	ὁδον	ἡμων	προς
Christ	may he direct	the	way	of us	to

ὑμας.
you.

This solemn ejaculation for the divine direction is addressed jointly to the God and Father, and to our Lord Jesus;* (so that here is good authority for offering up prayers to Christ, which some have lately opposed;) and the distinction of the persons is preserved (as in the last example) by again inserting the article ὁ before Κυριος, which had been omitted before Πατηρ. The apostle James also used the same mode of expression,

---

* This text is clearly a supplication to Christ for providential assistance; and, being addressed to him *jointly* with God the Father, most certainly amounts to *supreme worship*, because the direction of Providence belongs to God alone: so that prayer for it, addressed to Christ, were he merely a minister and dispenser of God's providence, and not also truly God, would be utterly unlawful: and more especially so if such an inferior dispenser of providence (one that was not truly God) was to be addressed jointly with the heavenly Father; for, that would be blasphemous.

James, 1:27.

θρησκεια	καθαρα	και	αμιαντος	παρα
Religion	clean	and	undefiled	before

Τω	Θεω	και	Πατρι	αυτη	εστιν,
the	God	and	Father	this	is,

επισκεπτεθαι	ορφανους	και	χηρας	εν
to visit	orphans	and	widows	in

τη	θλιψει	αυτων	
the	affliction	of them,	etc.

And there are at least a dozen other places, (viz. Rom. 15:6, 1 Cor.15:24, Gal. 1:4, Ephes. 5:20, Col. 1:3, and 12* and 3:17, 1 Thes. 1:3, 1 Thes. 3:13, 2 Thes. 2:16, James 3:9, [and] Rev. 1:6) wherein *"the God and Father"* is mentioned exactly according to this rule; and there is no exception or instance of the like mode of expression, that I know of, which necessarily requires a construction different from what is here laid down, EXCEPT the nouns be *proper names,* or *in the plural number*; in which cases there are many exceptions; though there are not wanting examples, even of plural nouns, which are expressed exactly agreeable to this rule.

As the examples which I have annexed to my first rule consist of texts, wherein the sense is so plain that there can be no controversy concerning the particular persons to whom the several nouns are applicable, it will be thought, I hope, that I have already cited a sufficient number of them to

---

* Some copies have not the words θεω και in this twelfth verse; but only τω πατρι τω ικανωσαντι; in which last case this verse affords an example only of the second rule.

authenticate and justify the rule. The there are several other texts wherein the mode of expression is exactly similar, and which therefore do necessarily require a construction agreeable to the same rule; though the present English version has unhappily rendered them in a different sense, and has thereby concealed, from the mere *English* reader, many striking proofs *concerning the Godhead* (περι "της Θεοτητος," Col. 2:9) of our Lord and Saviour, Jesus Christ.

The rules which follow are intended only to illustrate the *particularity* of the several sentences which fall under *the first rule*, by showing, in *other* sentences, the different senses that are occasioned by adding, omitting, or repeating, the article, as well *with* the copulative as *without* it.

RULE II.

A repetition of the article before the second noun, if the copulative be omitted, will have the same effect and power: for, it denotes a farther description of the same person, property, or thing, that is expressed by the first noun; as in the following examples:

Luke, 1:47.

και	ηγαλλιασε	το	πνευμα	μου	επι	τω
and	exulted	the	spirit	of me	in [upon]	the

Θεω	τω	Σωτηρι	μου
God	the	Saviour	of me

Luke, 2:26.

και	ην	αυτω	κεχρηματισμενον	ύπο	του
and	was	to him	having been communicated	by	the

Πνευματος	του	άγιου	
Spirit	the	holy,	etc.

John, 1:29.

ιδε	ό	αμνος	του	Θεου	ό	αιρων
behold	the	lamb	of the	God	the	taking

την	άμαρτιαν	του	κοσμου
the	sin	of the	world

John, 4:42.

οιδαμεν	ότι	ούτος	εστιν	αληθως	ό
we know	that	this one	is	truly	the

Σωτηρ	του	κοσμου,	ό	Χριστος
Saviour	of the	world,	the	Christ

John, 5:23.

ό	μη	τιμων	τον	'Υιον	ου	τιμα
the [one]	not	honoring	the	Son	not	honors

τον	πατερα	τον	πεμψαντα	αυτον
the	father	the [One]	having sent	him

John, 6:27.

εργαζεσθε	μη	την	βρωσιν	την
Work	not [for]	the	food	the

απολλυμενην,	αλλα	την	βρωσιν	την
perishing,	but	the	food	the

μενουσαν	εις	ζωην	αιωνιον,	ἥν	ὁ
remaining	to	life	eternal,	which	the

Ὑιος	του	ανθρωπου	ὑμιν	δωσει·	τουτον
Son	of the	man	you	will give;	this [one]

γαρ	ὁ	Πατηρ	εσφραγισεν	ὁ	Θεος
for	the	Father	sealed	the	God

This verse contains three examples.

John, 20:31.

Ταυτα	δε	γεγραπται	ἱνα	πιστευσητε
these	But	has[ve] been written	in order that	ye may believe

ὁτι	ὁ	Ιησους	εστιν	ὁ	Χριστος	ὁ
that	the	Jesus	is	the	Christ	the

Ὑιος	του	Θεου,	
Son	of the	God,	etc.

Heb. 13:20.

ὁ	δε	Θεος	της	ειρηνης	ὁ
the	Now	God	of the	peace	the [one]

αναγαγων   εκ   νεκρων   <u>τον</u>   ποιμενα

having led up   out of   [the] dead   the   shepherd

των προβατων   <u>τον</u>   μεγαν*   εν   αἱματι

of the sheep   the   great   in   blood

διαθηκης   αιωνιου,   <u>τον</u>   κυριον   ἡμων

covenant   of an eternal,   the   lord   of us

Ιησουν καταρτισαι   ὑμας,

Jesus   may he adjust   you,   etc.

This sentence also contains three [*sic*] examples.

* The apostle, in this text, expressly calls our Lord Jesus Christ "*the* Great SHEPHERD OF THE SHEEP," τον ποιμενα των προβατων τον μεγαν: and the apostle Peter entitles him "THE CHIEF SHEPHERD," ὁ αρχιποιμην, 1 Pet. 5:4, which compare with Psalm 23:1, "JEHOVAH *is my* SHEPHERD," and with Isaiah, 40:9,10,11; "*O Zion that bringeth good tidings,*" etc., "*say unto the cities of Judah, behold* YOUR GOD! *Behold the Lord* JEHOVAH *will come in mighty (power), and* HIS *arm shall rule for him.* He" (i.e. the Lord JEHOVAH) "*shall feed* HIS *flock like a* SHEPHERD: *he shall gather the lambs with his arm,*" etc., etc. To explain this still farther, the prophet Ezekiel foretold that "*all* shall have *one Shepherd,*" Ezekiel, 37:24. And Christ himself expressly acknowledged that *eminent pastoral* character, saying, "*I am the good Shepherd;*" ὁ ποιμην ὁ καλος, "and I know MY sheep and am known of MINE." (John, 10:14.) And a little farther (v. 27) our Lord mentions the *true mark* by which *his* flocks are known, viz. that *of hearing his voice:* (compare with 95th Psalm.) "*My sheep*" (said our Lord) "*hear my voice, and I know them; and they follow me, and I give unto them eternal life,*" etc., which power of *giving eternal life* cannot be an attribute of any person that is not truly God, and one with Jehovah or the heavenly Father, as in the 30th verse he is expressly declared to be "*I and my Father are one,*" ἑν εσμεν, *we are one*; in which brief expression both plurality and the unity of the two persons are unquestionably asserted.

(18)

GENERAL EXCEPTION.

Except when genitive cases depend on one another in succession; as,

2 Cor. 4:3. [2 Cor. 4:3,4]

ει	δε	και	εστι	κεκαλυμμενον		το	
if	But	and	is	having been hidden		the	

ευαγγελιον	ἡμων,	εν	τοις	απολλυμενοις
gospel	of us,	in	the [ones]	perishing

εστι	κεκαλυμμενον,	εν	ὁις	ὁ	Θεος
it is	having been hidden	in	whom	the	God

του	αιωνος	τουτου	ετυφλωσε	τα	νοηματα
of the	age	of this	blinded	the	thoughts

των	απιστων,	εις	το	μη	αυγασαι
of the	unbelieving,	to	the	not	to shine forth

αυτοις	τον	φωτισμον	του	ευαγγελιου
them	the	brightness	of the	gospel

τησ	δοξης	του	Χριστου	ὁς	εστιν	εικων
the	glory	of the	Christ	who	is	image

του	Θεου	του	αορατου
of the	God	of the	invisible

And, again, Coloss. 2:2.

ἱνα	παρακληθωσιν	ἁι	καρδιαι	αυτων
in order that	may be comforted	the	hearts	of them

συμβιβασθεντων	εν	αγαπη	και	εις
being joined together	in	love	and	for

παντα	πλουτον	της	πληροφοριας
all	riches	of the	full assurance

της	συνεσεως,	εις	επιγνωσιν	του
the	of understanding	for	full knowledge	of the

μυστηριου	του	Θεου	και
mystery	of the	God	and

Πατρος	και	του Χριστου	
Father	and	of the Christ,	etc.

RULE III.

And the omission of the copulative between two or more nouns (of the same case) of personal description or application, even without the article before the second noun, will have the same effect: viz. will denote a farther description of the same person, property, or thing, that is expressed by the first noun; as in the following examples.

Rom. 2:19,20.

Πεποιθας	τε	σεαυτον	ὁδηγον	ειναι
having persuaded	-	thyself	a guide	to be

τυφλων,	φως	των	εν	σκοτει,
of blind [persons]	a light	of the [ones]	in	darkness

παιδευτην	αφρονων,	διδασκαλον	νηπιων,
an instructor	of foolish [persons]	a teacher	of infants

εχοντα	την	μορφοσιν	της	γνωσεως
having	the	form	of the	knowledge

και	της	αληθειας	εν	τω	νομω
and	of the	truth	in	the	law

Ephes. 5:20, 21.

Ευχαριστουντες	παντοτε	ὑπερ	παντων	εν
giving thanks	always	for	all things	in

ονοματι	του	Κυριου	ἡμων	Ιησου
name	of the	Lord	of us	Jesus

Κριστου,	τω	Θεω	και	Πατρι·
Christ	to the	God	and	Father;

ὑποτασσομενοι	αλληλοις	εν	φοβω *
being subject	to one another	in	fear

Χριστου
of Christ

* Εν φοβω Χριστου. In the modern printed editions the reading is εν φοβω Θεου, but in the Complutensian and several of the oldest editions it is εν φοβω Χριστου; as also in the Alexandrian and other old MSS as well as the ancient versions, and the citations of the Fathers: for which see Wetstein's Testimony. Now compare this expression (εν φοβω Χριστου) with 1 Pet. 2:17. τον θεον φοβεισθε, τον βασιλεα τιματε: and also with 2 Kings, 17:35 and 36. "Ye shall not fear" (rendered by the seventy ου φοβηθησεσθε) "other gods; but JEHOVAH, who brought you out of the land of Egypt, etc., him shall ye fear."

Tit. 1:1.

Παυλος,	δουλος	Θεου,	αποστολος
Paul	a slave	of God,	apostle

δε	Ιησου	
and	of Jesus	etc.

1 Tim. 1:1.

Παυλος	Αποστολος	Ιησου	Χριστου
Paul	apostle	of Jesus	Christ

κατ᾽	επιταγην *	θεο	σωτηρος	ἡμων,
according to	a command	of God	saviour	of us

και	κυριου	Ιησου	Χριστου	της	ελπιδος
and	of Lord	Jesus	Christ	the	hope

ἡμων
of us

RULE IV.

Yet it is otherwise when the nouns are not of personal description or application; for, then they denote distinct things or qualities: as,

* Here the *command of Christ* is mentioned jointly with the command of *God* himself; which is a mode of expression never used concerning any other man, but the *Man Christ Jesus* our Lord, *"by whom are all things:* (1 Cor. 8:66 [*sic* - 8:6], Hebrews 1:2, John 1:3, Col. 1:16) and *"by whom all things consist."* Col. 1:17.

1 Tim. 1:2.

Τιμοθεω,	γνησιω	τεκνω,	εν	πιστει,
To Timothy	a true	child	in	faith,

χαρισ,	ελεος,	ειρηνη	απο	Θεου
grace,	mercy,	peace	from	God

Πατρος	ἡμων,	και	Χριστου	Ιησου
Father	of us	and	Christ	Jesus

του	κυριου	ἡμων
the	Lord	of us

2 Tim. 1:2; Titus 1:4 *; see also 2 John 3.

εσται	μεθ'	ὑμων	χαρις,	ελεος,
will be	with	us	grace,	mercy,

ειρηνη,	παρα	Θεου	Πατρος,
peace	from	God	Father

και	παρα	Κυριου	Ιησου	Χριστου
and	from	Lord	Jesus	Christ

του	'Υιου	του	Πατρος,	εν	αληθεια
the	Son	of the	Father,	in	truth

και	αγαπη.
and	love.

* In all these three texts, and in 2 John, 3, there is a manifest supplication made to *Christ, jointly with God the Father, for grace, mercy, and peace*; all divine gifts. The supplications, therefore, must necessarily be considered as acts of *supreme worship to both.*

(23)

RULE V.

And also when there is no article before the first noun, the insertion of the copulative kai before the next noun, or name, of the same case, denotes a different person or thing from the first: as in the following examples.*

Ephes. 4:31.

Πασα πικρια, και θυμος, και
All bitterness and anger and

οργη, και κραυγη, και βλασφημια,
wrath and clamor and blasphemy

αρθητω αφ᾽ ὑμων, συν παση κακια,
let it be removed from you with all evil,

This last sentence contains four examples of the fifth rule.

* Note by the Author. [In the former editions of this little work, as well as in the original MS. of it, the 1st verse of the general epistle of St James was cited as the *first* example of this 5th rule; viz. Ιακωβος Θεου και Κυριου Ιησου Χριστου δουλος [Ed.- "James of God and of Lord Jesus Christ a slave"]. For, the author had supposed that the words Θεου και Κυριου, having no article before the first substantive, must here denote two different persons, according to the general idiom of similar expressions throughout the New Testament, when the copulative is inserted without the article: but, having since read the just reasons and ample testimonies produced for a contrary interpretation of *this particular text*, in one of the *six letter*s addressed to himself (p. 114 to 120) by the Rev. Mr. Chr. Wordsworth, (for, it would be injustice to conceal that gentleman's name, since his merit and indefatigable labor, in forming that learned work, have been so generally approved,) he is thereby convinced that this text may with more propriety be placed among the *exceptions* to the fifth and six rules than as an *example* of the fifth; and he hath,

(24)

2 Cor. 1:2.

Χαρις	ὑμιν	και	ειρηνη	απο	Θεου
Grace	to you	and	peace	from	God

Πατρος	ἡμων	και	Κυριου	Ιησου	Χριστου
Father	of us	and	Lord	Jesus	Christ

Ephes. 1:2, Gal. 1:3, Philem. 3.

Ephes. 6:23*

Ειρηνη	τοις	αδελφοις	και	αγαπη
Grace	to the	brothers	and	love

μετα	πιστεως	απο	Θεου	Πατρος
with	faith	from	God	Father

και	Κυριου	Ιησου	Χριστου
and	Lord	Jesus	Christ

[Cont.] therefore, withdrawn it from the examples, notwithstanding that Mr. Wordsworth hath produced (in p. 120) the authority even of an ancient Greek writer for that example, in the same sense that was first cited in this place as denoting two distinct persons, contrary to Mr. Wordsworth's own opinion of it. "But there is *one* Greek writer" (says he) "who has clearly adopted the other interpretation. It is Œcumenius, in his commentary. Ιακωβος Θεου και Κυριου Ιησου Χριστου δουλοσ ταις δωδεκα κ.τ.λ. Θεου μεν του Πατρος, Κυριου δε του ὑιου, etc. Vol ii. p. 441.]

* The supplication for *grace* and *peace* jointly from God the Father, and from the Lord Jesus Christ, in all these five texts last cited, are so many unquestionable instances of *prayer* and *supreme worship* to CHRIST, as

(25)

Except the numerical adjective ἑις precedes the first noun; in which case the copulative και will have the same effect that is has between two nouns where only the first is preceded by the article, agreeably to the first rule; as,

Ephes. 4:6.

Ἑις	Θεος	και	πατηρ	παντων,	ὁ
one	God	and	Father	of all,	the [One]

επι	παντων,	και	δια	παντων,	και
over	all,	and	through	all,	and

εν	πασιν	ὑμιν
in	all	you

RULE VI.

And as the insertion of the copulative και *between nouns of the same case,* without articles, (according to the fifth rule,) *denotes that the second noun expresses a* different person, thing, or quality, from the preceding noun, *so, likewise,* the same effect *attends the copulative when each of the nouns are preceded by articles:* as in the following examples.

John 1:17.

ὁ	νομος	δια	Μωσεως	εδοθη	ἡ	χαρις
the	law	through	Moses	was given	the	grace

και	ἡ	αληθεια	δια	Ιησου	Χριστου	εγενετο
and	the	truth	through	Jesus	Christ	became

[Cont.] being a free disposer of those divine gifts *jointly* with his Almighty Father; agreeably to what I have already remarked above on 1 Thess. 3:11, and Titus 1:1.

John 2:22.

ὁτε	ουν	ηγερθη	(Ιησους)	εκ	νεκρων,
when	then	he was raised	Jesus	out from	dead,

εμνησθησαν	ὁι	μαθηται	αυτου,
remembered	the	disciples	of him

ὁτι	τουτο	ελεγεν	αυτοις,	και
that	this	he said	to them,	and

επιστευσαν	τῃ	γραφῃ,	και	τῳ	λογῳ
they believed	the	scripture,	and	the	word

ᾧ	ειπεν	ὁ	Ιησους
which	said	the	Jesus

John 11:44 [Ed.- John 11:43-44]

φωνῃ	μεγαλῃ	εκραυγασε	(Ιησους)	Λαζαρε,
voice	with a great	he cried out	(Jesus)	Lazarus,

δευρο	εξω.	Και	εξηλθεν	ὁ	τεθνηκως,
come	out.	And	came out	the [one]	having died,

δεδεμενος	τους	ποδας	και	τας	χειρας
having been bound	the	feet	and	the	hands

κειριαις,	και	ἡ	οψις	αυτου
with bandages,	and	the	face	of him

σουδαριῳ	περιεδεδετο
with a napkin	had been bound round

Col. 2:2. [Ed.- Col. 2:2-3]

εις	επιγνωσιν	του	μυστηριου		του	Θεου
for	full knowledge	of the	mystery		of the	God

και	Πατρος,	και	του	Χριστου,	εν
and	Father,	and	of the	Christ,	in

ᾧ	εισι	παντες	ὁι	θησαυροι	της
whom	are	all	the	treasures	of the

σοφιας	και	της	γνωσεως	αποκρυφοι
wisdom	and	of the	knowledge	hidden

2 Tim. 1:5

ὑπομνησιν	λαμβανων	της	εν	σοι
recollection	taking	of the	in	thee

ανυποκριτου	πιστεως,	ἡτις	ενῳκησε
unfeigned	faith,	which	indwelt

πρωτον	εν	τη	μαμμη	σου
first	in	the	grandmother	of thee

Λωϊδι	και	τη	μητρι	σου	Ευνεικη·
Lois	and	the	mother	of you	Eunice;

πεπεισμαι	δε,	ὁτι	και	εν	σοι
I have been persuaded	and,	that	also	in	thee

1 Pet. 4:11.

ἱνα	εν	πασι	δοξαζηται	ὁ Θεος	δια
in order that	in	all	may be glorified	the God	through

Ιησου	Χριστου,	ᾧ	εστιν	ἡ	δοξα
Jesus	Christ	to whom	is		the glory

και	το	κρατος	εις	τους	αιωνας
and	the	might	unto	the	ages

των	αιωνων.	Αμην.
of the	ages.	Amen.

Except distinct and different actions are intended to be attributed to *one and the same person*; in which case, if the sentence is not expressed agreeably to the three first rules, but appears as an exception to this sixth rule, or even to the fifth, (for, this *exception* relates to both rules,) the context must explain or point out plainly the person to whom the two nouns relate: as in 1 Thess 3:6.

Αρτι	δε	ελθοντος	Τιμοθεου	προς	ἡμας
now	But	coming	Timothy	to	us

αφ᾽	ὑμων	και	ευαγγελισαμενου	ἡμιν
from	you	and	announcing good news	to us

την	πιστιν	
of the	faith,	etc.

And also in John 20:28.

Και	απεκριθη	ὁ Θωμας,	και	ειπεν
and	answered	the Thomas	and	said

αυτω	ὁ	Κυριος	μου	και	ὁ
to him	the	Lord	of me	and	the

Θεος	μου
God	of me

If the two nouns (viz. ὁ Κυριος and ὁ Θεος) were the leading nominative substantives of a sentence, they would express the descriptive qualities or dignities of *two distinct persons*, according to the sixth rule; but, in this last text, two distinct divine characters are applied to *one person* only; for, the context clearly expresses *to whom the words were addressed by Thomas*: which perspicuity *in the address* clearly proves, likewise, the futility of that gloss for which the Arians and Socinians contended; viz. that Thomas could not mean that *Christ was his God*, but only uttered, in his surprise, a solemn exclamation or ejaculation to God. The text, however, expressly relates that our Lord first addressed himself to Thomas:

[Ed.- John 20:27-28]

ειτα	λεγει	τω	Θωμα,	φερε	τον
then	he said	to the	Thomas,	bring	the

δακτυλον	σου	ὡδε,
finger	of thee	here, etc.

και	απεκριθη	ὁ Θωμας	και	ειπεν
and	answers	the Thomas	and	says

αυτω
to him

(that is, without doubt, to Jesus,)

ὁ	Κυριος	μου,	και	ὁ	Θεος	μου
the	Lord	of me	and	the	God	of me

So that both these *distinct* titles (for, they are plainly mentioned as *distinct*) were manifestly addressed, αυτω [Ed.- "to him"], to that *one person, Jesus*, to whom *Thomas replied*, as the text expressly informs us. The language is so plain, when the whole context is considered, that the Socinian perversion of it is notorious. See also 1 Cor. 1:24.

Χριστον	Θεου	δυναμιν	και	Θεου	σοφιαν*
Christ	of God	power	and	of God	wisdom

and Acts 2:36. † There are also other examples of this exception which clearly prove that *Christ is God*: as

Rev. 1:17,18.

Μη	φοβου.	εγω	ειμι	ὁ	πρωτος	και
Not	fear	I	am	the	first	and

* Example of the exception to the fifth rule.

† Note lately added by the Author. [See also James 1:1, the text withdrawn from the examples of the fifth rule for the reasons assigned by the learned and Rev. Mr. Chr. Wordsworth, in his six letters to the author, p. 114 to 120.] [Ed.- see Extracts for reviews of "Six Letters."]

ὁ εσχατος, και ὁ ζων.* και εγενομην
the last, and the living and I became
[one]

νεκρος, και ιδου ζων ειμι εις τους
dead, and behold living I am unto the

αιωνας των αιωνων· αμην. Και εχω
ages of the ages: Amen. And I have

τας κλεις του ᾳδου και του θανατου *
the key of the Hades and of the death

These are the words of him whom John saw, ὁμοιον Ὑιῳ ανθρωπου [Ed. - Rev. 1:13: "one like a son of man"], with a two-edged sword proceeding out of his mouth; which was undoubtedly a representation of the Λογος, or word of God, as this declaration alludes plainly to his death and resurrection.

Εγενομην νεκρος, και ιδου ζων ειμι
I became dead, and behold living I am

And again in the second chapter, ver. 8 [Ed. - Rev. 2:8]:

ταδε λεγει ὁ πρωτος και ὁ εσχατος,*
These things says the first and the last,

(and the same infallible mark of distinction is added to prove which of the divine persons is here to be understood,) ΟΣ εγενετο νεκρος, και εζησεν [Ed.-"who became dead and he lived"]. Now, though the explanation which Grotius has given us of these titles (ὁ πρωτος και ὁ εσχατος) is

* Example of the exception to the sixth rule.

certainly true when applied to Christ, yet it does not appear to be the *whole truth*, or the full meaning that ought to be attributed to these titles, either in the Revelation or elsewhere; for, they have a manifest reference to the supreme titles of *the Almighty* in the first chapter and eight verse, (which also contains examples of this exception,) [Ed.- Rev. 1:8]

εγω	ειμι	το	A	και	το	Ω,*	λεγει
I	am	the	Alpha	and	the	Omega	says

ὁ	κυριος,	αρχη	και	τελος,†	ὁ	ων
the	Lord,	beginning	and	ending,	the [one]	being

και	ὁ	ην,*	και	ὁ	ερχομενος,	ὁ
and	the [one]	was,	and	the [one]	coming,	the

παντοκρατωρ.
Almighty.

And, in the 22nd chapter, 13th verse, where these titles, το A και το Ω, and manifestly, by the context, to be understood as the title of Christ, we find them explained by these other titles, ὁ πρωτος και ὁ εσχατος, [Ed.- "the first and the last"] to which Grotius has attributed a much inferior and less comprehensive meaning. [Ed.- Rev. 22:13]

Εγω	ειμι	το	A	και	το	Ω,*	αρχη
I	am	the	Alpha	and	the	Omega,	beginning

και	τελος,†	ὁ	πρωτος	και	ὁ	εσχατος.*
and	ending,	the	first	and	the	last.

* Example of the exception to the sixth rule.
† Example of the exception to the fifth rule.

And as I have shown in my Tract on *the Law of Nature*, etc. p. 270 and 271, that these titles, *"the first and the last,"* are ancient titles of *Jehovah*, in the Old Testament, to declare his *eternal existence*, there can be no just reason for giving them an inferior sense when they are applied to Christ, who was truly *Jehovah*, as a variety of texts demonstrate. [*Law of Nature*, p. 248 to 345.]

Another example of the exception to the fifth rule occurs in the Rev. 20:2.

τον	οφιν	τον	αρχαιον,	ὁς	εστι
the	serpent	the	old,	who	is

διαβολος	και	σατανας
Devil	and	Satan

These are two different names, or appellatives, attributed (by the explanatory words ὁς εστι) to the same Old Serpent.

THE END OF THE RULES.

The various uses of the article and copulative, expressed in the five last rules and their exceptions, must amply illustrate, to every attentive reader, the difference and particularity of those sentences which fall under the first and principal rule; and therefore I may now proceed with more confidence to point out several important corrections that ought to be made in our common translation of the New Testament, if the several sentences, which fall under the *first rule,* be duly weighed and considered; — corrections which may be fairly defended, I apprehend, by the authority of the several examples from which those rules were formed.

EXAMPLES.

Of sentences which fall under the FIRST RULE, *and are improperly rendered in the English version.*

EXAMPLE I. 2 Pet. 1:1.

εν	δικαιοσυνη	του	Θεου	ἡμων	και	σωτηρος
in	righteousness	of the	God	of us	and	Saviour

ἡμων	Ιησου	Χριστου.
of us	Jesus	Christ.

As the article του is not repeated before the next descriptive noun, σωτηρος, it is manifest that both the nouns are to be referred to one and the same person; and, therefore, in order to turn it into an intelligible English phrase, the *proper name* to which the *two descriptive nouns* refer ought to be placed first, as, "By the righteousness of Jesus Christ, OUR GOD and OUR SAVIOUR." Among the various readings collected by Curcellæus, it appears that in some copies the word ἡμων was not repeated after σωτηρος, and I have by me twenty different editions (including those of Erasmus, Stephens, Dr. Mill, Bengelius, etc.) which follow that reading: viz. εν δικαιοσυνη του Θεου ἡμων και σωτηρος Ιησου Χριστου, in which case, a literal rendering into English will sufficiently express the sense of the Greek without transposing the proper name; viz. *"Through the righteousness of our God and Saviour, Jesus Christ."* The sense and purport, however, is exactly the same in both the readings; and, in the old English editions, has generally been expressed in the terms required by my first rule; viz.

"In the righteousness that cometh of oure God and Saviour, Jesu Christ." (fol edit. 1549.)

"Through the righteousnesse of our God and Saviour, Jesus Christ." (12 mo edit. 1595.)

"By the righteousnesse of our God and Saviour, Jesus Christ." (4to edit. 1599.) [Ed.- quarto edit. 1599.]

"The righteousness of Jesus Christ, our God and Saviour." (margin of the folio edit. 1611.)

And even in the margin of our present version the proper reading is "of our God and Saviour," manifestly referring both titles to one person. The learned Beza also remarks, on the words of this text,

"Ista necesse est conjunctim legamus quia unicus est articulus, ut copiosius diximus Tit. ii.13. Itaque continet etiam hic locus manifestum divinitatis Christi testimonium."

The two nouns are referred to Christ also in the Syriac version. There seems, therefore, to be ample authority for my first rule.

EXAM. II. Titus, 2:13.

επιφανειαν της δοξης του μεγαλου Θεου
appearance   of the glory of the great God

και σωτηρος ἡμων Ιησου Χριστου.
and Saviour of us Jesus Christ.

In some few copies a comma is inserted between Θεου and και, but without authority. The above-mentioned note of Beza, upon this text, is too long to be inserted here at length, and therefore I must refer you to the author himself. He insists, however, that these two titles do not refer to two distinct persons, because the article is omitted before the second. In the present English version it is rendered — " *the glorious appearing of the great God and our Saviour Jesus Christ:*" but so great is the difference between the idiom of the Greek tongue and that of the English, that a *literal translation* will not always express the same sense without some little transposition in the order of the words; and, therefore, though the pronoun ἡμων is placed after the two descriptive nouns that are applicable only to *one* person and they are expressed in the Greek, yet the rendering of the said pronoun *in English* ought to be PREFIXED to the said descriptive nouns, in order to express the *same sense* in a proper English phrase; as, — *"the glorious appearing of OUR great God and Saviour, Jesus Christ."* — This is the rendering of the learned Hugh Broughton, according to a printed English Bible, corrected with a pen, in my collection. It might, indeed, be literally rendered without transposition of the pronoun; viz. *"the great God and Saviour OF US,"* instead of *"OUR great God and Saviour:"* but the latter is more agreeable to the general mode of expressing that pronoun in English. Thus Christ is not only entitled God, but even the *"great God"* according to the plainest grammatical construction of the text: and, indeed, if we duly weigh the evidence of his being really *Jehovah,* and *one with the Father,* [εγω και ὁ Πατηρ ἐν εσμεν, [Ed.- "I and the Father we are one"] the plural verb εσμεν ("we are") marking the plurality, or distinction of more persons than one, as much as the noun ἑν marks the *unity* of their existence,] he must necessarily be esteemed *"the great*

*God," * because there is but ONE GOD.* G. S.

* As we believe that three persons exist in one and the same God, we cannot believe any one of them to be less than God, without denying the unity of the Godhead. And, as each person is God, it follows that each must be the *great God.* Theophylact bears an explicit testimony of this conclusion in his commentary on St Paul's epistle to Titus, 2:13 "Που δε εισιν οι τον υίον ελαττουντες, και ουδε Θεον ανεχομενοι λεγειν; Ακουσετοσαν, ότι και Θεος εστι, και μεγας. Το δε μεγας επι Θεου λεγεται, ου κατα συγκρισιν την προς αλλον μικρον, αλλ' απολελυμενως, ώς φυσει αυτομεγαλου οντος." *Now what becomes of their objections, who degrade the dignity of the Son, not allowing him even the name of God? Let them learn from this passage, that he is not only God but our great God. He is called great God, not relatively, by comparison with another inferior God, but, absolutely, from his own native and essential greatness.* Whitby, in his note on the same passage of Titus, has given some very solid reasons for applying the terms μεγαλου Θεου to our Saviour. His words are: "Here it deserveth to be noted, that it is highly probable, that Jesus Christ is here styled the *great God*; first, because in the original the article is prefixed only before the *great God,* and therefore seems to require this construction, 'the appearance of Jesus Christ the great God and our Saviour.' Secondly, because as God the Father is not said properly to *appear*, so the word επιφανεια never occurs in the New Testament, but when it is applied to Jesus Christ, and some coming of his; the places, in which it is to be found, being only these, 2 Thess. 2:8, 1 Tim. 6:14, 2 Tim. 1:10, and 4:1,8. Thirdly, because Christ is emphatically styled *our hope, the hope of* our glory. Col. 1:27, 1 Tim. 1:1. And, lastly, because not only all the ancient commentators on the place do so interpret this text, but the Ante-Nicene fathers also; Hippolytus (Antichrist. Sect. 64) speaking of 'the appearance of our God and Saviour Jesus Christ;' and Clemens of Alexandria (ad Gent. p. 5,6) proving Christ to be both God and Man, our Creator, and the author of all our good things, from these very words of St Paul." *Vid. tract. de vera Christi deitate,* pp. 44, 45. Hammond, also, in his literal marginal version, translates επιφανειαν της δοξης του μεγαλου Θεου και σωτηρος ήμων Ιησου Χριστου, thus, "the appearance of the glory of our great God and Saviour Jesus Christ."

EDITOR.

The remainder of this letter is lost. The author had not leisure to copy the original letter before he sent it to the gentleman to whom it was addressed, and therefore he requested him to return it as soon as he had perused and considered it; but the gentleman neglected this request; and the author, after several years solicitation, obtained only a part of the letter, (as far as is here copied,) and the remainder (which was written on a separate half-sheet) he has never yet been able to recover. He had however a short memorandum of the several texts, which were explained in the latter part of the letter; and, having since had favorable opportunities of examining the said texts, and of copying them very accurately from the ancient Alexandrian manuscript in the British Museum, he has been enabled to make some short remarks on the versions of all the said texts, which may serve as a sufficient Supplement to this imperfect letter. Some notes have been added to this printed copy which were not in the original letter.

G. S.

EXAMPLES

TO THE

GRAMMATICAL RULES

OF

CONSTRUCTION, &c.

EXAMPLE I.

ACTS, 20:28.

Προσεχετε   ουν   έαυτοις   και   παντι   τω
Take heed   therefore   to yourselves   kai   to all   the

ποιμνιω   εν   ᾧ   ὑμας   το πνευμα   το
flock   in   which   you   the Spirit   the

άγιον   εθετο επισκοπους   ποιμαινειν   την
Holy   placed   overseers   to shepherd   the

εκκλησιαν   του   Θεου,   ἡν   περιεποιησατο
church   the   God,   which   he purchased

δια   του ιδιου   άιματος.
through   of the own   blood.

The warning of the apostle Paul to the presbyters of the church of Ephesus, which is thus rendered in the common English version: "Take heed therefore unto yourselves, and to all the flock over which the holy Ghost hath made you overseers, to feed the church of God, which he hath purchased with his own blood."

In the Alexandrian MS and a few other MSS instead of του Θεου, which is the most general reading, the word Κυριου is substituted; but many old MSS have both words, του Κυριου και Θεου,* whereby the text is brought within the construction of the 1st rule, and should be rendered, — "To feed the church of the *Lord, even of God*, which he hath purchased with *his own blood.*"

Though there is no word in the Greek to correspond with this word *"even,"* so as that it might be deemed *a literal rendering*, yet this English word is frequently used by our translators to express the *identity of person*, when a copulative, in the Greek text, joins a second substantive (i.e. of *personal* description without an article) to the former substantive, preceded by an article, agreeably to the first rule, as in Romans, 15:6.

τον Θεον και Πατερα
the   God   and Father

---

* Note lately added by the Author. [Three of the ancient Greek MSS in the Caesarian Library at Vienna, and 1 Sclavonian MS (cited in the Vienna edition of 1787,) have this reading; and it is inserted in the margin of the elegant 12mo edition of 1553, printed by John Crispin. For the same reading Dr. Mill refers to fifteen MSS.]

and 1 Cor. 15:24.

τω   Θεω   και   Πατρι
the   God   and   Father

both of which are rendered, — *"God, even the Father,*
(instead of the literal rendering, *the God and Father,*) that the
identity of person may be the more obvious. See also 2 Cor
1:3:

ευλογητος   ὁ   Θεος   και   πατηρ   του
Blessed   the   God   and   Father   of the

Κυριου   ἡμων   Ιησου   Χριστου, ὁ
Lord   of us   Jesus   Christ,   the

πατηρ   των   οικτιρμων,   και   Θεος   πασης
Father   of the   compassions,   and   God   of all

παρακλησεως.
comfort.

This sentence contains two successive examples of the first
rule, and is rendered, "Blessed be God, *even* the father of our
Lord Jesus Christ, the father of mercies, and the God of all
comfort." See also James, 3:9; τον Θεον και Πατερα. 1
Thess. 3:13; του Θεου και Πατρος ἡμων. 2 Thess. 2:16;
και ὁ Θεος και Πατηρ. Besides these six examples,
wherein the word *even,* in the English version, expresses the
copulative, there are also 13* *other examples of the first rule*
in the New Testament: i.e., altogether 19 examples respecting
our *heavenly Father* alone; and therefore the 9 examples of

* Viz. 2 Cor. 11:31. Gal. 1:4. Ephes. 1:3 and 4:6, and v. 20. Philip,
4:20. Col. 1:3, and 2:2, and 3:17. 1 Thess. 1:3, and 3:11. James, 1:27.
1 Peter, 1:3.

the same mode of expression, produced in this and the following pages, respecting the *Son and the holy Spirit*, ought certainly to be rendered in a *sense* suitable to the same uniform rule of construction, to express the *identity of persons,* because the same mode of grammatical expression is used in them all.

EXAMPLE II.

EPHESIANS, 5: 5.

— ουκ	εχει	κληρονομιαν	εν	τη
— not	has	inheritance	in	the

βασιλεια	του	Χριστου	και	Θεου
kingdom	of the	Christ	and	God

In the common English version the sentence is rendered, *"No whoremonger,* etc., *hath any inheritance in the kingdom of Christ, and of God."* As if two persons had been mentioned in the original text; but, as the part of the sentence above cited is the generally-approved reading of the printed *Greek copies,* and as this reading is confirmed by the Alexandrian MS and by all other Greek MSS of known authority, it affords an unquestionable proof against the *apostasy of the Socinians* in their *denial of divine honor to our Lord the Christ, or Messiah,* who, according to the idiom of the Greek tongue, is in this text expressly entitled Θεος, "GOD," though the proof does not appear in the English version. Let it be remarked that the two substantives of personal description, Χριστου and Θεου, are joined by the copulative και, and that the article του precedes the first, and that there is not article before the word Θεου, whereby, according to the *first rule,* both titles are *necessarily* to be applied to *one* and the same person, and (if literally rendered in English) should be, — "hath no inheritance in the kingdom of *the Christ and God."* But this literal rendering does not sufficiently express the necessary doctrine of the Greek, that the *Christ* is *also God:* and therefore to help the English idiom, and to accommodate the rendering more strictly to the true meaning of the Greek, the name of *Jesus,* which is necessary to be *understood,* might very fairly be inserted in *italic,* or between hooks, as a parenthesis, to supply the necessary sense of the Greek; as, "in the kingdom of (Jesus) the Christ and God:" or else to be rendered, "in the kingdom of Christ, (even) of God," as recommended in the first example.

EXAMPLE III.

PHILIPIANS, [*sic* - PHILIPPIANS,] 3:3.

ἡμεις	γαρ	εσμεν	ἡ	περιτονη,[*sic*-περιτομη,]
we	For	are	the	circumcision,

ὁι	πνευματι	Θεου	λατρευοντες,	και
the [ones]	spirit	of God	worshipping,	and

καυχωμενοι	εν	Χριστω	Ιησου,	και
boasting [glorying]	in	Christ	Jesus	and

ουκ	εν	σαρκι	πεποιθοτες.
not	in	flesh	trusting.

This is rendered, in our common version, — "For we are the circumcision, which worship *God* IN the Spirit, and rejoice in Christ Jesus, and have no confidence in the flesh."

In the London Polyglott, and many other valuable editions, the reading is όι πνευματι Θεω, but in the Alexandrian MS * it is όι πνευματι Θεου, which seems to be the true reading; because the other is so unusual an expression, that the generality of translators have forced a construction which the context itself cannot fairly bear, even if the dative case, Θεω, were admitted to be the true reading, unless another word, the preposition εν, be also added to it before πνευματι, as in John, 4:23, and Rom. 8:9, where the sense, which they have applied to this text, was really intended: but, without this addition, (as we may fairly judge by those examples,) the literal rendering ought to be, "We are the circumcision, *who worship the Spirit God.*" Whereas they have commonly rendered it as if the preposition εν was really inserted in this text before the dative, πνευματι, as in the two examples before cited; viz. *"Qui Spiritu Servimus Deo,"* or *"Qui Spiritu colimus Deum:"* or, as in the Syriac version, *"Qui Deo Servimus in Spiritu:"* (Syr.) or, as in the common English version, *"Which worship God in the Spirit."* But there is no such preposition in the Greek. The difficulty therefore of rendering the common reading, (Θεω,) without supposing this addition of EN to be understood before πνευματι, proves that the reading of the Alexandrian MS in this text is really to be preferred; όι πνευματι Θεου*

* Many other ancient and valuable Greek MSS as Dr. Mill has testified, have this reading, Θεου, but Augustine testified, that, in his time, *all or almost all Greek* copies, and many Latin, had the reading "SPIRITUI DEI." *"Plures enim Codices etiam Latini sic habent, qui* SPIRITUI DEI *servimus,* GRÆCI *autem* OMNES, AUT PENE OMNES. *In nonnullis autem exemplaribus* LATINIS *invenimus non* SPIRITUI DEI SERVIMUS," *sed* "SPIRITUI DEO SERVIMUS. *Sed qui in hoc erravit et authoritati graviori cedere detrectavit, etc."*

In Wetstein's edition the word Θεου is subjoined with this mark §, to denote the preferable reading.

(45)

λατρευοντες, *"who worship the spirit of God,"* [1] whereby the apostle and Timothy, as an example to the church at Philippi, assert their profession, that they pay *divine honor to the spirit of God,* and *that they glory in Christ.*

EXAMPLE IV.

2 THESS. 1:12.

Κατα	την	χαριν	του	Θεου	ημων	και
According to	the	grace	of the	God	of us	and

Κυριου	Ιησου	Χριστου.
Lord	Jesus	Christ.

This, in the common English version, is rendered (very erroneously) as if two distinct persons were mentioned, viz.

[1] [Ed. note- The dative, πνεύματι, is viewed by some as an instrumental as "by spirit" thus the translation *"the ones worshipping by the Spirit of God . . ."* or as a locative as, "in spirit" thus *"worshipping in the Spirit of God . . ."* However, R.C.H. Lenski in *The Interpretation of St Paul's Epistles to the Galatians, to the Ephesians, and to the Philippians, (Minneapolis: Augsburg Publishing House, 1961),* p. 831, supports Sharp's translation. Lenski writes, "The correct reading is 'God's Spirit' and not the dative 'God' (A.V.). But the dative 'God's Spirit' is not instrumental, the means 'by' which *we* worship (R.V.). If that were the force, the very inferior reading πνεύματι Θεῷ would be preferable: worship God with (our) spirit (compare A.V.), John 4:24: 'in spirit and truth.' The Scriptures never say that we use the Holy Spirit as a means for worship or for anything else. On the other hand, we challenge the statement that the Scriptures never present the Holy Spirit as the object of our worship; this is sometimes extended to include also our Lord Jesus Christ. This claim is Arian. Right here Paul writes: 'We are the ones worshipping God's Spirit.'"]

"according to the grace of our God and the Lord Jesus Christ." But, if two distinct persons had really been intended to be expressed, as (by innumerable examples of the grammatical construction of sentences, for the accurate distinction of persons peculiar to the Greek tongue, used in the Greek Testament, from which the preceding rules were formed) may be demonstrated, the article would have been repeated (according to the sixth rule) after the copulative and before the second substantive κυριου. For, it is manifest that the insertion of the comma, in some Greek copies, after ἡμων, is a modern interpolation; because the expedient of breaking sentences into small divisions or particles by commas, to preserve the necessary distinctions, was not anciently used (nor likely to have been used) by the ancient writers of the Greek tongue, who were accustomed to much more accurate distinctions in their various peculiar modes of grammatical expression, specified in the six preceding rules.

Whole sentences are, indeed, distinguished, in the oldest Greek MSS by a single point place at their end, sometimes towards the top of the line, sometimes in the middle, and sometimes towards the bottom; but, apparently, no distinction of time has been intended by any of these three different modes of placing the point, for, they are all placed, indiscriminately, to the most obvious and full termination of sentences; and, therefore, we may be assured, that, in all these three different modes of placing them, they were originally intended only as periods to conclude the sentences: so that, when we find them in the place of commas, to distinguish merely the parts or particles of a sentence, there is great reason to suspect that they have been the additions of later times.

In the Alexandrian MS the text before us is awkwardly divided by one of these points, placed after the word ἡμων, which point, for the reason before given, must necessarily be deemed a *period,* and which did not exist in the original text of the sacred penman.

The intention of the transcriber, or interpolator, by adding this point to the text, (for it cannot justly be attributed to the original writer,) has been probably to make a distinction of person; as if *two* persons had been named in the text instead of *one*, in like manner as the comma is added after the word *God*, in the English version, *without any authority.*

But the necessary grammatical construction of the whole sentence taken together detects the interpolator, and demonstrates the absurdity of supposing that any such point ever existed in the original text, because the words, which are severed by the supposititious period, cannot form a grammatical sentence (according to the ordinary modes of expression used in the Greek tongue) by themselves alone; so that the obvious sense of the context demonstrates their necessary connection with the preceding words *in one entire sentence:* and demonstrates, also, at the same time, the ignorance and fallacy of the interpolator, who attempted to make two sentences of it by inserting a full period.

If literally rendered, it ought to be, — "according to the grace of the God and Lord of us, Jesus Christ:" but, more in the idiom of our own language, it might be justly rendered, "according to the grace of Jesus Christ, our God and Lord." In either way the necessary doctrine of our Lord's divine nature, manifestly intended to be expressed in the original, is duly retained in the proposed version.

EXAMPLE V.

1 Tim. 5:21.

Διαμαρτυρομαι	ενωπιον	του	Θεου	και
I solemnly witness	before	the	God	and

Κυριου	Ιησου	Χριστου	και	των
Lord	Jesus	Christ	and	the

εκλεκτων	αγγελων,	ινα	ταυτα	φυλαξης
chosen	angels	in order that	these things	thou guard, etc.

This, in the common English version, is rendered, — "I charge (thee) before God, and the Lord Jesus Christ, and the elect angels, that thou observe these things, etc."

The word Κυριου* is omitted in the Alexandrian MS where the reading is ενωπιον του Θεου και Χριστου Ιησου. And, as no points are inserted between the substantives, we have the testimony even of this MS for a clear declaration that *Jesus* is God as well as *Christ*: and, after the next copulative, which connects the mention of different persons, according to the sixth rule, the adverb ενωπιον, (*before,*) though not expressly repeated, is plainly to be understood; as, -- "*I charge*" (thee), "*before the* GOD *and* CHRIST, *Jes*us," (or, rather, *before Jesus, the God and Christ,*) "*and*" (before) "*the elect angels, that thou observe these things.*" Thus far the testimony of the Alexandrian MS. -- But, according to the commonly-received text of the Greek, it ought to be rendered, in the English idiom, "*I charge* (thee), *before Jesus Christ, the* GOD *and* LORD, *and* (before) *the elect angels, etc.*"

* Note lately added by the Author. [The *Author* acknowledge himself to be under great obligation to a judicious and learned writer in the

(49)

[cont.] *British Critic* for a very important correction of what was written under this fifth example, and also under the 6th, in the former editions of this little book; as well as for his general candor in reviewing, and declaring a decided favorable opinion upon, the whole design of it. (See the *British Critic* for July 1802; and also Remarks on a former edition of the year 1798, in the 15th vol. of the *British Critic*, p. 70.)

Under this fifth example the *Author* had inadvertently inserted the word Χριστου instead of Κυριου, in his report respecting the omission of a word in the Alexandrian MS. And, in his remarks on the sixth example, he had reversed this mistake by mentioning Κυριου instead of Κριστου [*sic* - Χριστου]. As soon as the Author had read, in the *British Critic,* the detection of these two errors, he immediately referred to the original paper on which he at first, many years ago, had carefully delineated the several texts in question from the Alexandrian MS in the exact form of the letters and length of the lines; and, finding therein the true reading of the MS as stated in the *British Critic*, he was the more surprised to observe that he himself had inadvertently transposed (in his subsequent remarks drawn from the very same paper) the word Χριστου for Κυριου, and Κυριου for Χριστου!

These were involuntary errors of the *Author himself* alone, for which the very worthy and learned Editor (who relied on the *Author*'s examination of the MS) is not at all responsible: and the *Author* himself, though he had so accurate a delineation of the texts, from the MS in his possession, did not observe this unaccountable transpositon that he had made of the two words, in his remarks, until he was apprised of the mistake by the learned writer in the *British Critic*, for which he thinks himself under very great obligation.   *G.S*

An extract from the *British Critic* is inserted in the Appendix, not only for the better illustration of the subject in question, but, also, more particularly, to set forth, in terms more satisfactory to the *Author* than any expressions he himself could suggest, the indefatigable labor, learning, and judicious criticism, of the Rev. Mr. *Chr. Wordsworth*, of Trinity-College, Cambridge, in his six letters to G.S. on the subject of this book; by which the doctrine, particularly of the *first rule*, has been so amply confirmed. For the same reasons are added extracts also from the ingenious and learned observations on both these works, (the Remarks by G.S. and Mr. Wordsworth's six letters to him upon them,) which were published in the *Christian Observer* for July, 1802, and in the *Christian Guardian* for December, 1802, and also in the *Orthodox Churchman's Magazine and Review* for February, 1803.]

EXAMPLE VI.

2 Tim. 4:1.

Διαμαρτυρομαι   ουν   εγω   ενωπιον   του
I solemnly witness   then   I   before   of the

Θεου   και   Κυριου   Ιησου   Χριστου
God   and   Lord   Jesus   Christ

του   μελλοντος   κρινειν   ζωντας   και   νεκρους,
the   being about   to judge   living   and   dead,   etc.
[one]

(*Geneva Edit.* 1620.)

In the common English version this is rendered, "I charge (thee) therefore before God, and the Lord Jesus Christ, who shall judge the quick and the dead, etc."

In the Greek of this text, as it is commonly printed, the article του is repeated before Κυριου, which, so far, affords an excuse for the present English version in placing the comma after the word *God*, to denote *two* distinct persons, according to the sixth rule; but, in the Alexandrian MS and several other old copies, *[where the reading is ενωπιον του Θεου και Χριστου Ιησου] the article του is *not* repeated after the copulative before Χριστου: so that the expression is similar, in effect, to the declaration of our Lord's *divine nature*, by the same apostle, in the preceding example, viz. 1 Tim. 5:21. In some printed editions the word Κυριου is also omitted, but, in the Geneva edition of 1620, with Scaliger's notes, the word Κυριου is inserted and the article

---

* [ ] Correction and addition by the Author.

του omitted,* whereby the title Θεου, (God,) must necessarily be construed in such a manner that it may be clearly understood, in all versions, to be expressly applied to *Christ*, as it really is in the original. The transcriber or interpolator of the Alexandrian MS however, being aware of this doctrine, has endeavored to pervert it by adding a full period after the word Θεου, as Θυ· But this *period* is unquestionably supposititious, because the words before and after the period are *not two distinct sentences*, but obviously portions only of *one entire sentence*, which must necessarily be construed together, according to the ordinary rules of expression in the Greek tongue, as I have remarked on a preceding example; whereby a second substantive of

---

* Note lately added by the Author. [The expression being exactly the same as that which is generally allowed to exist in the preceding example, viz. ενωπιον του Θεου και Κυριου Ιησου Χριστου, 1 Tim. 5:21. And the Author has lately discovered several other editions of the Greek Testament which have this reading, and thereby confirm the truth of this 6th example; though it must be allowed, at the same time, that *not even one* of the several *editors* understood the text in its proper *grammatical sense*, because they have all (without any authority) placed commas after Θεου, in order to distinguish *two persons*, contrary to the necessary grammatical construction of the Greek text. Two of these editions (in the Author's possession) have Montanus's interlineary Latin version. They are both in 8vo, though of different sizes, the one having four more lines in each page than the other; but the title-pages of both being lost their respective dates cannot be known. (There are several other 8vo editions with the same interlineary version, but which have a *different* reading in this place, viz. the common reading with the article inserted in the second place after the copulative; and two such editions are also in the Author's collection.) The fourth printed authority, which the Author has found, in favor of his sixth example is the Vienna edition of 1787, printed from an ancient MS in the Imperial Library at Vienna. The title of it is, *"Novum Testamentum ad Codicem Vindebonenfem Græce expressum. Varietatem Lectionis addidit Franciscus Carolus Alter Professor Gymnasii Vindebonensis."* At the end of the second volume (for it consists of two very thick 8vo volumes) are added the various readings of seven other ancient Greek MSS all containing the Epistles, (besides the MS from which the edition was formed,) which have been separately collated with

personal description, *without an article before it*, joined by a copulative to a preceding substantive of the like nature, and in the same case, *with an article before it*, must necessarily denote a farther description of the same person, expressed by the first substantive; (whenever there is an article before the first substantive and none before the second;) so that the insertion of the *period* in the Alexandrian

[cont.] this edition; and the variations are distinctly and separately stated, under the proper titles of each MS in the Appendix. Two, only, of all these eight MSS have, in this text, the article του repeated in the second place after the copulative, (viz. του Θεου και του Κυριου, etc.) Another of them has the same reading exactly as the Alexandrian MS του Θεου και Χριστου Ιησου: and, therefore, by the omission of the article in the second place before Χριστου, doth also, equally with that MS confirm the doctrine of my sixth example. And all the other five MSS (which likewise contain this Epistle) must necessarily be allowed to have the other more correct reading for which I contend, viz. του Θεου και Κυριου Ιησου Χριστου: because no difference or variation from that reading, in the printed edition, is noted in any other of the seven separate collations of ancient MSS that have been distinctly compared with it, except in the three that are first mentioned above.

Though the insertion of the article in the second place is undoubtedly the most common reading in all the printed editions, (for fifty-nine out of sixty-four printed Greek Testaments, in the possession of the Author of this little work, have this reading,) yet several of the most learned Editors of these fifty-nine editions, that have adopted it, have, at the same time, warned us that there are various readings in this text, viz. *Bishop Walton, Curcellæus, Bishop Fell, Dr. Mill, Henry Wetsten*, and *John Jac. Wetsten.* The latter cites no less than six ancient MSS (besides several versions,) which have not the reading του Κυριου. (N.B. His mark for a deficiency is a short line thus —; and he has expressed this various reading, in his note on the text, as follows: "του Κυριου.] — A C D a prima manu. F G. 31. *Editio Vulg. Copt. Œthiop. Basilius* Eth. 89 *Hilarius.*") And consequently we must understand that all these six MSS have the same reading as the first of them, A, by which mark he refers to the *Alexandrian* MS wherein, though the words του Κυριου are indeed omitted, yet the proper effect of this omission ought to be at the same time remarked, viz. that the article του is not repeated after the copulative, in the second place, before the next noun Χριστου: so that the

MS* after Θεου is utterly vain, because the *copulative* sufficiently proves the *connection* of the two substantives in

[cont.] expression, in all these six MSS must be equally declaratory of our Lord's divine nature, as in the former example (the fifth) from 1 Tim. 5:21. To the evidence of these six MSS must be added that of *one* of the Imperial MSS at *Vienna,* mentioned above.

John Jac. Wetsten (my authority for the evidence of the five of the ancient MSS which agree with the Alexandrian MS in the particular reading of the text last-mentioned) has also acknowleged [*sic*-acknowledged] a very considerable degree of evidence in favor of the other reading, which I have adopted as my sixth example; (though he was, apparently, of a very different opinion from myself respecting the propriety of it;) for, he cites no less than three MSS (besides the Geneva edition, which I have quoted) wherein the reading, as he asserts, *is without the article in the second place.* See his note, vol. ii, p. 364, viz. "του secundo loco.] — E. 4. 52. Editio Genev. The short line — is his mark, or sign, for a deficiency, as signified in his prolegomena, p. 222; (last line but one;) viz. " — in V. L." (i.e. in Variis Lectionibus,) *"notat voces, quibus appositum est, in codd. citatis non legi."* And E is his mark for the ancient *Basil* MS. But he must have made some mistake respecting the two other MSS 4 and 52, for he has described them in his prolegomena (p. 46 and 51) as containing the *four Gospels,* without making any mention of their having also the *Epistles*; so that these two MSS have probably been cited, by mistake, instead of some other MSS which he had known to contain the same reading as the *Basil* MS and the *Geneva* Edition.

But, even if we set aside these two supposed MSS yet as it appears that five out of the eight ancient MSS in the Imperial Library at *Vienna,* as well as the ancient *Basil* MS cited by Wetsten, and also four printed editions, have this reading; and that six other MSS agree with the Alexandrian MS in a different reading of this text, which bears equal testimony to *the divinity of Christ*; the Author hopes it will be allowed that all this united evidence affords some reasonable ground of justification for his having cited this text as his sixth example.]

* Note lately added by the Author. [And also the insertion of commas after Θεου, in the four printed editions, is equally vain, and proves only that the Editors were not aware of the proper grammatical construction of the text.]

one clear sentence, and the omission of the article before the second substantive induces the necessity of applying the same grammatical construction, whereby alone the due distinction of persons is so peculiarly maintained in the Greek tongue, and *not by points.* The text should therefore be rendered, — "I charge (thee,) therefore, before the God and Lord, Jesus Christ, etc." Or, rather, (to render the doctrine more obvious in the English idiom,) — " I charge (thee,) therefore, before Jesus Christ, the God and Lord, who shall judge the quick and the dead, etc." And thus the text in the two last examples will perfectly accord as the uniform expressions of the same apostle asserting, in both* the *divinity of his Lord and Saviour,* by whom he had been personally summoned to bear his testimony to the gentiles, as being an eye and ear witness of his *glorious majesty.*

Our Socinian Sadducees, who have impiously entitle our Lord *"a mere man,"* and *"nothing but a man,"* and *"simple human nature,"* will not be able to digest this necessary doctrine until they humble themselves to receive instruction from the holy scriptures.

---

* Note lately added by the Author. [This seems to have been the opinion also of the learned *Bengelius*, that both these texts had originally the same mode of expression. For, in his Gnomon, he remarks, on the text of the former example, (1 Tim. 5:21) και Κυριου et Domini, "Articulus non additur, cum tamen mox addatur de angelis. Ergo *Dei* appellatio et *Domini* ad unum pertinet subjectum. Conf. tamen II. Tim. iv. I, κυριου non habet lectio vetusta." To restore this *ancient reading without the article in the second place*, there seems to be ample authority by the testimony of the MSS and editions which I have cited, in addition to *the similarity of expression*, by the *same apostle*, in 1 Tim. 5:21.]

EXAMPLE VII.

TIT. 2:13.

— Προσδεχομενοι την μακαριαν ελπιδα και
— expecting   the   blessed   hope   and

επιφανειαν της δοξης του μεγαλου Θεου
appearance   of the   glory   of the   great   God

και σωτηρος ἡμων Ιησου Χριστου
and   saviour   of us   Jesus   Christ

The present version of these words, in the English testament, is, — "Looking for that blessed hope, and the glorious appearing of the great God, and our Saviour Jesus Christ." This text (though the next in order, according to the usual mode of arranging the books of the New Testament) has already been produced as the second example in the preceding letter. I have since, however, examined the Alexandrian MS and find that it agrees exactly with the above citation of this text, except that a point has been added in the MS after the word Θεου or Θυ. On which it is necessary to observe, that the same remarks are obviously applicable to this superfluous and absurd addition of the point or *period,* that I have made on the texts 2 Thess. 1:12; and 2 Tim. 4:1, in the fourth and sixth examples of this tract. For, as the proper effect or purpose of *periods* is to separate words into *distinct sentences*, it is obvious that the words, which follow the supposititious period in this text, are incapable of a grammatical construction without reference to the preceding words connected by the *copulative*: and therefore the *note of separation* (a period) cannot possibly have been intended by the inspired writer. This testimony, therefore, of the sacred text, in favor of our Lord's *divine nature*, ought not to be withheld from the mere English reader.

I am persuaded that our modern Socinians would not have made so much clamor, about *the necessity of a new translation,* had they been aware that a more close and literal rendering of the original text (even in passages which had escaped their calumnious charges of *corruption,* and their arrogant attempts at imaginary *correction)* must necessarily cut up their favorite system by the roots.

The text in question, if the truth of the original be duly regarded, must inevitably be rendered, *"Expecting the blessed hope and appearance of the glory of our great God and Saviour, Jesus Christ."*

EXAMPLE VIII.

2 Pet. 1:1

— εν	δικαιοσυνη	του	Θεου	ημων	και	σωτηρος
— in	righteousness	of the	God	of us	and	Saviour

Ιησου	Χριστου
Jesus	Christ

Which, in the common English version, is thus imperfectly rendered, — *"through the righteousness of God and our Saviour, Jesus Christ."**

This text, though the *eighth* in order, according to the proper order of the books, was *the first* example cited in my

---

* Note lately added by the Author. [But in the margin (with the usual mark of reference to the Greek text, viz. Gr. when a more literal version is given) it is properly rendered, — *"of our God and Saviour."*]

letter; and I have only to remark farther, that the Alexandrian MS perfectly agrees with the present common approved reading in the Greek text. In Dr. Woide's printed copy of the said MS there is a point inserted after the word δικαιοσυνῃ, which is not in the MS but that is manifestly a merely-accidental typographical error.

The Reverend Mr. Crutwell has remarked (in his useful editon of the English Bible with Bishop Wilson's Notes) that the words rendered in our present version, viz. *"of God and our Saviour, Jesus Christ,"* were rendered, *"of our God and Saviour, Jesus Christ,"* in the versions of Wickliff, Coverdale, Matthews, Cranmer, in the Bishops (Bible,) (the) Geneva, (the) Rhemish, (Bibles,) and by Doddridge, Wesley, Scattergood, and Purver; which is altogether a noble testimony of both ancient and modern time against the *Socinian impiety.* The *English* reader should undoubtedly be informed of the true meaning of these words in a proper *English* idiom, as — *"Through the righteousness of Jesus Christ, our God and Saviour:"* — which is agreeable to a literal rendering into Latin by the late learned Dr. Thomas Mangey, Prebendary of Durham, viz. — *"Jesu Christi Dei et servatoris nostri."*

EXAMPLE IX.

Jude 4.

—	και	τον	μονον	Δεσποτην	Θεον
—	and	the	only	Master	God

και	Κυριον	ἡμων	Ιησουν	Χριστον	αρνουμενοι.
and	Lord	of us	Jesus	Christ	denying.

This, in the common English version, is imperfectly rendered — *"and denying the only Lord God, and our Lord*

Jesus Christ."

I made a transcript of this text, several years ago, from the Alexandrian MS which I copied, or rather drew, letter by letter, in size and shape as exactly as the eye could discern. In this transcript the word Θεον is omitted, as in the MS but I did not, at that time, perceive that there was any point or mark after the word Δεσποτην, and I was therefore much surprised, afterwards, in comparing the said transcript with the elegant edition of my late very worthy and respectable friend, the Rev. Dr. Woide, (who printed a copy of the New Testament from the Alexandrian MS with new types, in imitation of the letters of the MS) to find that he had inserted a point, in his new edition, after the word Δεσποτην. I was very confident that I could not discern any such point, when I examined the MS; and yet, as I entertained the highest respect and esteem for the veracity and accuracy of Dr. Woide, (of which he was, indeed, truly worthy,) it was necessary to have this matter properly explained; and I was rendered perfectly aware, by Dr. Velthusen's account of his examining an ancient MS that the faint line and marks in the very old MSS are liable to bear different appearances, according to the different degrees of light in which they are seen.

I therefore took the first opportunity, afterwards, of going once more to examine the MS; and, on a more close inspection, I perceived, indeed, the *faint* mark which occasioned Dr. Woide's insertion of the period in his edition; but being afterwards assisted by the worthy librarian, the Rev. Mr. Harper, in a still more attentive and accurate examination of the mark with a magnifying glass, I was satisfied that it had not been intended for a period, but only for a short *line of connection,* because it is nearly three times as long as it is broad.

But if any person, from the authority of Dr. Woide's edition, should be still inclined to suppose that it is really *a point,* I must request them carefully to consider what I have before remarked on the fourth, sixth, and seventh, examples in this tract, respecting the addition of *points* in Greek manuscripts; and also concerning the more accurate modes of grammatical distinction in the Greek tongue, which rendered the smaller points, or *particles of time,* (such as semicolons and commas,) absolutely unnecessary in the *Greek scripture*; and, in addition thereto, let him observe, particularly on the text before us, that a point in that place, after Δεσποτην, (in the middle of the sentence, between the accusative noun and verb,) is utterly inconsistent with grammar and common sense; and though the word Θεον has been omitted in the Alexandrian MS (perhaps for the same reason that some men would wish to prove the insertion of the point after Δεσποτην,) yet, happily, neither of these alterations would at all affect or injure the manifest testimony of the apostle Jude *to Christ's almighty power and divinity,* for — "the only potentate and Lord of us, Jesus Christ," is equivalent to a full declaration of *Christ's divinity,* as well as of his almighty power; and, with respect to the insertion of the *supposed point,* they must perceive, if they duly consider the text, that the words Δεσποτην and κυριον cannot (consistently with the necessary grammatical sense of the Greek, and the usual modes of expression, or idiom of that language) be separated either by points or construction, so as to be applied to two different persons, because the article is not repeated after the copulative, before κυριον: so that *Christ alone* was unquestionably that — *"only potentate,"* or *Sovereign Lord,* who was denied by the *lascivious persons,* against whom the apostle Jude bore testimony of their *reprobacy,* and of their having *denied the Lord,* who had *redeemed them.* Dr. Hammond's rendering of the text before us may, therefore, be conscientiously maintained, viz. *"our only Master, God, and*

Lord, Jesus Christ, * *making"* (says he) *"those three the several attributes of Jesus Christ."* — But as the Doctor has been pleased to add, afterwards, — *"And this interpretation proceeds upon that way of punctuation which is ordinarily retained in our copies, there being no comma after* Θεον, *etc."* I am obliged to protest against *that reason, for the other reasons* already given; and to insist, that the grammatical construction of the Greek text is, of itself, our sufficient and best warrant to justify that *literal rendering.*

But the applying to Christ this Supreme title, — *"the only potentate, God"* (and, also, in a former text, the *Supreme* title of — *"the great God"*) may, perhaps, induce some persons to conceive that this grammatical system of construction, if admitted as a rule, for all texts, in which the same mode of expression renders it applicable, will sometimes prove rather too much, and may be liable to favor a modern sect of *Unitarians,* who have adopted the *Sabellian* notions of the late Baron Swedenborg, and who assert, that — *"Jesus Christ is the only God;"* that is, they understand this in so peculiar a sense, that they do not seem properly to acknowledge the *personality* of *the holy spirit,* any more than a very opposite sect of *Unitarians* do, the modern Socinians, who impiously assert (in the opposite extreme to that of the *Swedenborgians*) that *"Jesus Christ was a mere man, and nothing but a man,"* according to one of their teachers, and — *"simple human nature,"* according to another: and some of them have even presumed to charge the members of the church of England with idolatry† because they pay *the divine honor that is due* to their Lord and Saviour, and to the *holy spirit,* their — *"other comforter."*

---

* Viz. in the margin of the text; and repeated in his Annotations, p. 850, with the remainder of this quotation.

† This unjust charge of idolatry against the unquestionable principles of the *ancient catholic church,* professed by the *church of England,* affords

So that both these sects of *Unitarians* (as well as their *Unitarian* brethren, the *Mahometans*) are, by mistaken notions of the *divine unity*, seduced from perceiving and acknowledging the declarations, throughout the holy Scriptures, of the unquestionable existence of *three* divine persons in *one* only divine natur*e, or Godhead.* The old Arians (though their sect was probably represented by that *"fallen star"* which opened the *"bottomless pit"* for the emission of the *armed locusts* of the Arabian heresy, *more*

[cont.] a notable screen to the Latin church, by indiscriminately confounding all the due distinctions whereby a charge of *idolatry* is applicable; and this should teach us to be aware of what we should have to expect on the removal of all tests and restraints from such indiscriminate teachers; and, likewise, from all other sectaries (as much as from the *pontifical hierarchy*, seated on the *throne of the dragon*) who do *not* regulate their faith and practice by the plain doctrines of the holy Scriptures. For, indeed, no man is justly entitled to have a vote or share in the legislature of this or any other *Christian* nation, unless he (at least) professes to regulate his *principles of action* by the *two first foundat*ions of ENGLISH LAW, viz. *natural* and *revealed religio*n, to which (as being *two witnesses of God) universal obedience* is due, so that no statute of parliament can be *valid,* nor any other law, custom, or practice, *sufferable,* if it be *at all* inconsistent with either of *these two indispensable foundations.* For, without these, MEN retain, indeed, the form, but not the *dignity*, of MAN; because they are subject to the impulse of *spirits,* inimical to the *nature of man*; and are, thereby, liable to be rendered, in disposition and practice, the most noxious of *beasts,* even — *"a generation of vipers;"* and, therefore, *the knowledge of our own* NATURE, *and of the principles of action in* MAN, *what they are and what they ought to be,* (which, by the Scriptures alone, is revealed to us,) is the first and most essential branch of *philosophy,* whatsoever our modern skeptical *philosophers* may think to the contrary; for, how should men be on their guard against any *invisible enemies*, of whose very existence they are ignorant? — But by the holy Scriptures we are informed, that — *"the prince of the power of the air worketh in the children of disobedience;"* — and, certainly, wherever this *Satanical inspiration* manifestly takes place among *men,* their *descriptive title* cannot be more accurately expressed than in the terms which our Lord himself (as well as John the Baptist, before him) applied to the haughty *strictly Unitarians* than themselves*) allowed, indeed, that *Christ was God,* yet they supposed him to be so, in *an inferior degree;* by which they unwarily acknowledged a *superior* God, and an *inferior* God: i.e., *more* Gods than *one,* contrary to the *true Unitarian doctrine* of *the primitve churches,* which always held and asserted *the unity of God*

[cont.] skeptics whom they opposed, — *"a generation of vipers,"* (Matthew 12:34;) and *"serpents:"* (Matthew, 23:33:) expressly alluding thereby to the *Satanical inspiration* by which they became the *children,* or *generation,* of the *old Serpent,* as our Lord plainly warned them at another time: — *Ye are of* YOUR "FATHER THE DEVIL — *and the lusts of* YOUR FATHER *ye will do: — he was a* MURDERER *from the beginning, and abode not in the truth, etc."* Men, therefore, who will not be limited by the *two first foundations of English law,* are unworthy to be admitted to an equal participation of *civil rights* in any free *Christian* state whatever; because *true liberty* cannot be maintained without that *perfection of law* which arises *only* from these *indispensable rules of action.*

They are *indispensable,* because we can have no hope that our *constitutional* establishment of *natural* and *religious rights* (to *"the glory of God, peace on earth,"* and *"good will towards men"*) can possibly be maintained, if such persons are admitted to a share of *legislative* authority, who do not acknowledge the *only foundations* on which, alone, that happy *constitution* is built.

* Since I wrote the above remark, respecting the *Mahometans* and *Arians,* a more striking accomplishment of the prophecy, respecting the *fallen star that opened the bottomless pit,* has occured to me, in the character of *Nestorius,* Archbishop of Constantinople and metroplitan of the Greek church, whose doctrine was, in effect, still *"more Unitarian than"* that of *Arius*; for, the consequences of his denying the miraculous birth of our Lord, and asserting that — *"Christ born of the Virgin Mary was not the Son of God;"* must necessarily be, that he was — *"a mere man,"* and — *"nothing but a man,"* according to the openly-declared notions of our modern Socinians, which, in this point, is strictly *Mahometan!* With this false and *antichristian* doctrine *"the third part of the rivers and fountains of water"* (viz. the sources of *the nations* and the *people* of the *Greek* Empire, the *third* great monarchy) was *embittered* and prepared for the *scorpion*-like scourge of *Mahometan* tyranny.

(like the church of England to this day) as much as they held it necessary to acknowledge the *three divine persons:* both of which doctrines are inevitable and indispensable while we profess to regulate our faith by the testimonies of the holy Scriptures, as handed down to us, without presuming to exercise the Socinian expedient of lopping off, or altering, (as a supposed *corruption* or *interpolation,*) every text of Scripture that opposes the system or set of notions that we happen to have adopted.   And, therefore, the *true Unitarian* Christian, who acknowledges but *one God, one Jehovah, one divine nature,* (Θεοτης,) or *Godhead,* and at the same time, nevertheless, is convinced, that *three divine persons* are really

[cont.]   On account of this blasphemous doctrine, *Nestorius* was deposed (by the judgement of a great counsel of his *peers,* the *Christian bishops*) from his dignity as *Archbishop* of the greatest city (at that time) in Christendom, and from being *metropolitan,* as it were, of *the Greek Empire,* (the *third* great monarch;) and, therefore, he might truly be said to have *fallen* from the highest elevation of ecclesiastical dignity; so that no prophetical type could more amply prefigure this rejection than — *"the fallen star from heaven,"* — the heaven or *firmament* of the then amply *established* episcopal authority throughout the Roman empire.   And the *Unitarian* doctrine of this *fallen star* (I mean *Unitarian* in the *Mahometan* and *Socinian* sense of that term) seems also to have been the very *"key,"* whereby *"the bottomless* pit" was opened to let out the noxious and diabolical vapor of *Mahometanism;* for, it is really the *leading* and first inclucated tenet in all the public professions of that baneful heresy.   And it is remarkable that a *Nestorian* monk, *Sergius,* professing the same blasphemous doctrine, (this —*"key of the bottomless pit"* forged by *Nestorius,*) should actually have been an assistant to *Mahomet,* in producing his pretended revelations; and it is still more remarkable, that all the *scorpion-like* scourges of *Mahometan* conquest (first, LAWLESS TYRANNY and the supression of all *popular rights*; secondly, ROBBERY and WAR notoriously sanctioned or authorized by this pretended religion against *all* nations and people that do not receive their doctrine; and, thirdly, the fatal *renewal* of the old *pagan* oppressions of

revealed to us under the title of *Jehovah** in the old
testament, and under the title of Θεος, or *God*, in the New
Testament; and that the *supreme attributes* of the DIVINE
NATURE are applied to each, in both Testaments; will, of
course, be aware, also, that each of these divine person must
necessarily be *"the great God"* and *"the only potentate,"* as
there is but *"one God,"* one only supreme power or *Godhead.*

[cont.] *slaveholding* and *slave-dealing,*† which had been happily
extinguished by the general influence of *Christian* benevolence) should
have completely pervaded all those eastern and southern regions of the
third Empire, wherever the doctrines of *Nestorius* had been previously
adopted, and had *embittered* the *rivers* and *fountains* of the waters, to
prepare them for this signal retribution, justly due to such antichristian
apostates, who deny the true *rock* on which the *Catholic church* is built,
viz. that *"Jesus is the Christ, the Son of the living God;"* or, as St. John
has expressed the *peculiar sonship*, or filiation, of Christ, viz. *"the* ONLY
BEGOTTEN SON, *which is in the bosom of the Father."* John, 1:18,
compare with ver. 14, and chap. 3:16 and 18.

All the arguments produced by the learned *Vitringa*, to prove that
A rius was the *fallen star,* are certainly much more applicable to *Nestorius*,
as being an *archbishop* and *metropolitan of the empire,* and therefore
more fitly prefigured by a *star.* And that the smoke from — "the
bottomless pit," which was let out by this *fallen star*, was really the mist
or diabolical darkness of *Mahometanism*, seems to have been fairly
proved by our learned countryman, Joseph Mede.

† Such diabolical enormities may surely be compared to the dark exhalations of — *"the
bottomless pit;"* and, therefore, our English promoters of *slave-holding* and *slave-dealing*
(who have carried these *Mahometan* oppressions to a greater excess even than the
Mahometans themselves) have ample reason to dread the approaching time of *divine
retribution,* when God will — *"destroy the destroyers of the earth,"* and shall cause those
that now — *"lead into captivity"* (and, surely, likewise, all their abettors) — *"to be led into
captivity!"*

* I need not, here, recite the proofs of these assertions because I have
already produced a great variety of examples, collected from the Old as
well as the New Testament, in my tract on the *"Law of nature and
principles of action in man,"* from p. 234 to p. 301.

So that the effect of my grammatical rule,* when applied to the two particular texts before-mentioned, (viz. Tit. 2:13, and Jude, 4) will not (in the opinion of such true Christians) seem to exceed the truth.

Though the apostle Paul asserted to the Colossians, (2:9,) concerning Christ, that *"in him dwelleth* ALL *the fullness of the Godhead,"* (της Θεοτητος,) "bodily," (σωματικως, a term of indisputable personality,) yet, surely, this was without the least disparagement to the supreme divinity of the *Almighty Father,* and of *the Holy Spirit,* because they are, also, necessarily included in the same Θεοτης, or *Godhead,* as there is but *one* God; and, therefore, as *"it pleased all fullness to dwell"* in the person of our *Lord Jesus Christ,* (Co. 1:19,) we may more easily comprehend why he required, *"that all"* (men) *"should honour the Son,* EVEN AS *they honour the Father;"* that is, undoubtedly, with *Supreme honour,* καθως, EVEN AS, or *according as, "they honour the father."* And our Lord said, expressly, *"he that honoureth not the Son* (that is, according to the measure before declared, "EVEN AS *they honour,"* or ought to honour, *the father) "honoureth not the father which hath sent him;* (John, 5:23;) and he also claimed expressly *to be glorified with the father himself. "And now, O father,* (said he,) "GLORIFY THOU ME WITH THINE OWNSELF, *with the glory which I had with thee before the world was;"* (John, 17:5;) thereby asserting both his *pre-existence* and *supreme dignity.* Christians, therefore, who humbly receive these and many other revelations of *Christ's divinity,* have the less difficulty in acknowledging the *doctrines of the ancient catholic churches* and the declarations of our *creeds.* But let all other men, likewise, who profess to believe in the *name of Christ,* earnestly inquire, in the *first* place, as the

---

* Compared with the concurrent reasons and testimonies quoted in the note, p. 35. EDITOR.

first means of progress to the true faith, where they are really "willing" (for this is given as the true proof of *faith*, εαν τις Θελη, [Ed.- "unless a person wills"]) to conform themselves to the *will of God*, as revealed in all the most obvious declarations and injunctions of holy Scripture, and more particularly to the purity, which is expressly called *"the will of God,"* viz. *the sanctification of their bodies,** which cannot otherwise be capable of becoming *"temples of the Holy Ghost:"* an indispensable state both of *body* and *mind* for all Christians to maintain; for, in that case, they may assuredly rely on God's absolute promise, through Christ, that *"if any one shall be* WILLING *to do* HIS WILL, *he shall know of the doctrine, whether it be of God, or whether I speak"* (said our Lord) *"from myself."* (John, 7:17.)

DEO SOLI GLORIA.

* "For this is the *will of God*, even your sanctification, that you should abstain from fornication: that every one of you should know how to possess his vessel in *sanctification* and *honour;* not in the lust of concupiscence, even as the Gentiles, which know not God: that no one should go beyond or defraud his brother, etc." 1 Thess. 4:3, 6.

APPENDIX.

I.

A TABLE OF EVIDENCES

OF

CHRIST's DIVINITY,

FROM

Dr. WHITBY's

COMM. on the NEW TESTAMENT

II.

A PLAIN ARGUMENT,

FROM THE

GOSPEL-HISTORY,

FOR THE

DIVINITY of CHRIST,

BY

THE EDITOR OF THE TWO FIRST EDITIONS.

Extract from Dr. Whitby's third Discourse,
subjoined to his Last Thoughts.

━━━

"THAT our Lord Jesus Christ is true God, as having true dominion over all things in heaven and earth delivered to him from the Father, and as having all divine excellencies which are necessary to enable him to exercise dominion while this world lasts, and at the close of the world to make manifest the secrets of all hearts, and to render to every man according as his works shall be, has been fully proved in my Last Thoughts, Sect. 4 and 5."

Discourse III. p. 143. subjoined to his *Last Thoughts.*

A TABLE

OF

EVIDENCES

OF

CHRIST's DIVINITY. *

THE divine nature of Christ may be proved,
I. From John, 1:1, 2, 3.   5:21, 22, 23.   8:58.   10:30.
12:41.   16:14, 15.   18:5.   20:28.   Luke, 1:43.

II. From his
    titles, he
    being

1. Jehovah, Rom 10:13.
2. God, Rom. 14:12.
   1 Cor. 10:9.   Heb. 1:8.
   and 3:4.
3. The true God,
   1 John 5:20.
4. God manifested in the
   flesh, 1 Tim. 3:16
5. The great God, Tit. 2:13.
6. God over all, blessed for
   ever, Rom. 9:5
7. The Lord of all,
   Rom. 10:12

* For the detail of these evidences see Dr. Whitby's Commentary on the
several passages here quoted.

The divine nature of Christ may be proved,

III. From the divine worship ascribed to him, he being the object of religious adoration and invocation, Rom. 10:13. Col. 3:24. 2 Thess. 3:16. Acts 7:59. Acts 9:14. Compare Matt. 4:10, with John 5:23, and Heb. 1:6.

IV. From the divine actions and attributes ascribed to him, he being:

1. Omniscient, John 2:25, 21:17. The searcher of all hearts, 1 Cor. 4:5.
2. Omnipotent, Philip. 3:21.
3. The raiser of all men from the dead, Col. 1:19.
4. Who raised himself from the dead, John 2:19, 10:18.
5. The Creator of all things, John 1:3. Col. 1:16. Heb. 1:2,10.
6. The upholder of all things, Col. 1:17. Heb. 1:3.
7. Who was in the form of God, and was God before he was made man, Philip. 2:6. John 1:1
8. In whom dwelt all the fullness of the Godhead bodily, Col. 1:19. 2:9.

A PLAIN ARGUMENT, *

FROM THE

GOSPEL-HISTORY,

FOR THE

D I V I N I T Y of C H R I S T.

QUESTION.

*F*OR what END did Christ COME INTO THE WORLD?

A. "Christ came into the world to save sinners." (1 Tim. 1:15.)

Q. *How do you mean "to save sinners?"*

A. To save them from the power of sin here, and the everlasting punishment of it hereafter.

Q. *How must we be saved from the everlasting punishment of sin?*

A. By Christ's DEATH. He was "manifested in the flesh," that is, was made man to DIE, and to be "THE PROPITIATION, for the sins of the whole world." "By his own blood Christ obtained redemption for us." (1 Cor. 15:3. 1 John 2:2. Heb. 9:12.)

Q. *How must we be delivered from the power of sin here?*

* Reprinted from the second Edition of *a Christmas Gift.*

A. By "the spirit of Christ." (Rom 8:9.) "For he came to destroy the works of the devil, to redeem us from all iniquity, and to purify unto himself a peculiar people zealous of good works." (1 John 3:8. Tit. 2:14.)

Q. *Must we not also use our own most earnest endeavors?*

A. Yes. We must "watch and pray" against all temptation to sin; (Matt. 26:41. Mark 13:13;) and study God's word that we may be sanctified by it. (John 17:17.)

Q. *Could no one save sinners but Christ?*

A. No. "There is none other name under heaven given among men, whereby we must be saved." (Acts 4:12.)

Q. *Could not Christ save sinners without dying for their sins?*

A. No.

Q. *Why could not man's redemption be accomplished without the death of Christ?*

A. Because it was the will of God, and fore-ordained by God, that Christ should die for the sins of the world.

Q. *How do you know that Christ's death was for-ordained by God?*

A. Because it was fore-told by the prophets.

Q. *Have you any other reason for believing that Christ's death was necessary for our salvation?*

A. I believe that without Christ's death there could have been no salvation, because we are assured, by the holy Spirit, in the words of St Paul, that "without shedding of blood there is no remission" of sins. (Heb. 9:22.)

Q. *Have you any other reason?*

A. Yes. The INCARNATION of Christ, that is, Christ's *being made man,* and *being born into the world,* seems also to be a proof that his death was necessary for our salvation. For he who "in the beginning was with God, and was God," was "made flesh," and "took upon him the form." that is, the nature, "and likeness, of man," on purpose, as it seems, that he might "*become* obedient unto death," (and thus might *be capable* of dying,) "even the death of the cross." (John 1:1. Philipp. 2:6, 7, 8.)

§. 2.

Q. *Where was Christ before he came into this world, and was manifested in the flesh?*

A. He was in Heaven. "He came down from Heaven. He was with God, his Father, before the world was, before the foundation of the world: he was in the bosom of his Father, and in his Father's glory." — (John 3:13. — 6:33, 62. — 1:1. — 17:5, 24. — 1:18. — 17:5.)

§. 3.

Q. *How was Christ's manifestation in the flesh made known to the world?*

A. By the message of an angel, who declared to Mary, his mother, and to Joseph, what manner of child it should be that should be born to her, and at his birth proclaimed him to certain shepherds.

Q. *Where was Christ born?*

A. In Bethlehem of Judea. (Matt. 2:1, 5, 6.)

Q. *Under what name was he made known?*

A. He was called JESUS, a Saviour, the Son of God, the Son of the Highest.

Q. *Who was the mother of Jesus?*

A. The Virgin Mary.

Q. *Was any prophecy fulfilled by the birth of Jesus Christ?*

A. Yes. "All this was done that it might be fulfilled, which was spoken of the Lord by the prophet, saying, behold a virgin shall be with child, and shall bring forth a son, and they shall call his name EMMANUEL, which, being interpreted, is GOD WITH US." (Matt. 1:22, 23. Isaiah, 7:14.)

§. 4.

Q. *What was Christ put to death for?*

A. For blasphemy, as the Jews thought it, in calling himself the Son of God.

Q. *In what did the Jews say the blasphemy consisted?*

A. In this, that he, being, as they supposed, a mere

man, called God his own Father, thereby declaring himself to be equal with God, and to be very God. (John 5:18. 10:33.)

§. 5.

Q. *What did Christ ever say of himself, which implied that he was God?*

A. He said that he was one with God, and partook of the glory of God, before the world was, that is, from all eternity.

Catechist. *Repeat the passage in which he said that he partook of the glory of God before the world was.*

A. "And now, O Father, glorify thou me with thine ownself, with the glory which I had with thee before the world was." (John 17:5.)

Q. *What did Christ ever say of himself, which implied that he was equal with God?*

A. He said that "he and his Father are one:" that "the Father had given all things into his hand:" that "what things soever the Father doeth, these also doeth the Son likewise:" that "the Father had committed all judgement to the Son, that all men should honor the Son, even as they honor the Father:" (John 10:30. — 3:35. — 5:19. — 5:22.)

§. 6.

Q. *Where do we find the first evidences of Christ's Divinity?*

A. In the ancient prophets, Isaiah, (7:14.) Jeremiah, (23:6.) and Daniel, (7:14.) where he is called "Immanuel," that is, GOD with us: "The Lord," that is, "JEHOVAH, our righteousness:" and his "dominion" is declared to be an "EVERLASTING dominion."

Q. *Who, in Christ's time, first bore testimony to his divinity?*

A. The angel, who at his birth proclaimed him to the shepherds, as "Christ, THE LORD:" The shepherds who made known this saying that was told them: And the Demoniacks, who acknowledged him to be THE SON OF GOD. (Mark 3:11.)

Q. *Who were the first witnesses to Christ's own testimony of his divinity?*

A. His enemies, the unbelieving Jews, both the people, and their rulers.

Q. *How are the unbelieving Jews witnesses to Christ's testimony of himself?*

A. By reporting and interpreting his words.

Q. *Do you call the unbelieving Jews earlier witnesses than the Apostles?*

A. Yes: because the apostles appear not to have known that Christ was God, till after his Resurrection and Ascension into heaven.

Q. *In what manner was the Divinity of Christ unfolded to the world in Christ's time?*

A. An angel proclaimed it at his birth; the shepherds reported it; the Demoniacks confessed it. Christ afterwards asserted himself to be God, by calling God his own Father, and himself the Son of God, in a sense, which implied, that he was equal with God, and was God; — so even his unbelieving hearers understood him: — the Jews condemned him to death for it: — the Apostles, after his Resurrection and Ascension, preached it to the world.

§. 7.

Q. *As Christ knew that this was the sense in which the Jews understood his testimony of himself, when they first charged him with blasphemy for it, — did he, at his trial, attempt to deny the charge?*

A. No: he admitted the charge, and confirmed it, and died for it; and appealed to the day of judgement as their future proof of it.

Q. *What are Christ's words?*

A. When "the high Priest asked him, and said unto him art thou the Son of the Blessed? Jesus said, I am; and *(as a proof that I am)* ye shall *(at the day of judgement)* see *(me)* the Son of Man, sitting at the right hand of power, *(that is, at the right hand of God,)* and coming in the clouds of heaven." (Mark 14:61, 62.)

Q. *If Christ had not been the Messiah, the Son of God, in the sense in which they understood him, would he not have undeceived them?*

A. If Christ had not been the Messiah, the Son of God, in the sense in which the Jews understood him, he would have undeceived them, to save his own like, and to free them from a very great delusion.

Q. But Christ was put to Death for calling himself the Son of God; what then do you conclude?

A. I conclude that Jesus Christ really was what they charged him with calling himself, THE SON OF GOD; and in the sense in which they understood him; that is, that he was EQUAL WITH GOD, and therefore was VERY GOD.

§. 8.

Q. You say that in the lifetime of Christ the Apostles appeared not to know that Christ was God: where do you find this?

A. It appears from their expecting a temporal deliverer instead of a spiritual one; and from their not knowing, till after the Resurrection and ascension of Christ, the end of his coming into the world.

Q. Where do you learn that, before the resurrection and ascension of Christ, his disciples did not know the end of his coming into the world?

A. I learn it from Christ's rebuke of St Peter. (Matt. 16:23.)

Q. Where do you learn that they expected a temporal deliverer?

A. I learn it from the acknowledgement of the two disciples, (who were going to Emmaus,) that their hopes of his being their deliverer were disappointed by his death; (Luke 24:21.) and from their inquiring of Christ, soon after his resurrection, if he would, at that time, restore the kingdom to Israel. (Acts 1:6.)

Q. What was their opinion of Christ after his resurrection and ascension into heaven?

A. Convinced partly by his resurrection from the dead, according to his promise that he would raise himself from the dead, and, fully instructed by the Holy Spirit after his ascension, they believed him to be "their Lord and their God," — "the Word made flesh," "God manifest in the flesh;" in whom "dwelt ALL the fullness of the Godhead bodily;" "Emmanuel," or, "God with us," — "the creator and upholder of all things," who "in the beginning" of all things, "was with God, and was God;" — "the true God and eternal life;" and "over all God blessed for ever." (John 20:28. 1:14. 1 Tim. 3:16. Col. 2:9. Matt. 1:23. John 1:3. Col 1:17. Heb. 1:3. John 1:1. — 1 John 5:20. Rom 9:5.*)

§. 9.

Q. Now, tell me, in few words, what you conclude from Christ's testimony of himself, as attested by the Jews of his own time, condemned by their rulers, but universally declared by the apostles.

A. I conclude that Christ, the Son of God, is one with God, and equal with God, both in nature, and power, and in glory, and therefore is very God. Christ asserted it; the Jews condemned him to die for it; he sealed his testimony with his blood. The apostles, partly convinced by his resurrection from the dead, and fully instructed by the Holy Spirit after

---

* Whatever difficulty may be found in the various readings of any of these passages, it must vanish in full light of their united evidence. To them we may confidently add the very important testimonies, which, in the preceeding [*sic* -preceding] remarks and examples, Mr. Sharp has most happily recovered from the erroneous constructions of the common English version.

his ascension into heaven, believed it, and preached it, and died for it.

§. 10.

Catechist. *The Jews, then, put Christ to death as an impostor and blasphemer; and yet Christians have believed in him, and worshipped him, as the Son of God, for almost eighteen hundred years. How do you account for this?*

A. It was the will of God that Christ should die for the sins of mankind. If the Jews had believed him to be the Son of God they would not have put him to death; — if he had not been put to death as he was he would not have "borne our sins in his own body on the cross;" that is, he would not have died for our sins, THE END FOR WHICH HE CAME INTO THE WORLD: — he would not have given that great and inestimable proof of the truth of Scripture, and of his own promises, which HE did, by rising from the dead: — and the Apostles would not have given that sure evidence of their own belief in Christ, (the ground and confirmation of OURS,) which THEY did, by dying for their crucified Lord and Master.

APPENDIX the THIRD.

═══════════════════════════════════════

CONTAINING

EXTRACTS

FROM

THE UNDERMENTIONED REVIEWS.

─────────────

The BRITISH CRITIC for January, 1800.

───────────── for July, 1802.

The CHRISTIAN OBSERVER for July, 1802.

The CHRISTIAN GUARDIAN for December, 1802.

The ORTHODOX CHURCHMAN for February, 1803.

EXTRACTS, Etc.

Extract from the BRITISH CRITIC for January, 1800. No. I. of vol. xv p. 70, art. xii.

"The design of the — — author, Mr. G. Sharp, is to demonstrate the divinity of our Saviour by showing, that, in several passages of the New Testament, translated as they ought to be, according to strict grammatical analogy, that article of our faith is expressly and positively asserted; though that assertion has, in our common version, disappeared for want of a correct rendering of the original. The six rules laid down for this purpose, the accuracy of which is proved in various ways, and particularly by the conduct of our translators on other occasions, we extracted at large in our notice of the Museum Oxoniense; but we shall now recur to them, because, in the table of contents here prefixed, we observe such an abstract of them, and of the examples, as to a scholar almost sufficiently explains the whole argument, its force, and application. The first rule is most important, being more extensive in its application than the rest; to this, therefore, we particularly call the reader's attention. It is thus stated in the table of contents, more briefly, but perhaps more clearly, than in the body of the work," etc.

After citing several examples of the first rule, the British Critic adds as follows, in p. 72, — "The examples here cited are by no means all that have the same tendency, but they are the most remarkable; and the remaining rules appear no less solid than the first. It should be observed, also, that, in several instances more than we have mentioned, the version recommended by Mr. G. S. has the sanction of several early translators and commentators."

And he concludes, in. p. 73, with the following observations on the appendix, viz. "The part subjoined to Mr. G. Sharp's remarks by the learned Editor, entitled 'a plain matter-of-fact argument,' etc., turns on this circumstance, that our Saviour was actually condemned to death by the Jews for blasphemy, in asserting his own Godhead; and that, instead of denying the circumstance, he confirmed it, and sealed his testimony with his blood. It is thrown into the form of question and answer, in order to be used in catechetical instruction, and is drawn up with great precision, clearness, and cogency of reason."

Remarks of the BRITISH CRITIC for July, 1802, No.1. of vol. xx. p. 15, art. iv.

Six Letters to Granville Sharp, Esq. respecting his Remarks on the uses of the Definite Article in the Greek Text of the New Testament.

"A great accession of authority, and, we trust, a proportionable increase of celebrity, will be given, by these acute and learned letters, to the Remarks of Mr. Granville Sharp on the Greek article, which, in our 15th vol. (p. 70,) we introduced to public notice, as of the highest utility and importance.* Those remarks, it must be recollected, are not merely of a philological nature, as the title might seem to imply; but, by means of a clear idiom and analogy of the Greek language, establish certain texts of the New Testament,

---

* "A second edition of Mr. Granville Sharp's Remarks has very recently been published by the original editor, Mr. Burgess, Presbendary of Durham, and is sold by Vernor and Hood, Rivingtons, and Hatchard. As, accidentally, we have not the former edition at hand, to make an accurate comparison between them, we shall not at present give a separate article on the new edition, nor at all, unless we find the alterations important."

as invincible barriers against the doctrines and subterfuges of Socinian teachers.

"This account applies principally to the first rule laid down in the Remarks, to which also the letters now announced refer; and we must remind or inform our readers, that by the natural and necessary operation of this rule are produced these texts: 'according to the grace of Jesus Christ, *our God* and Lord;' (2 Thess. 1:12;) 'waiting for the glorious appearance of *our great God and Saviour,* Jesus Christ;' (Titus, 2:13;) and some others of similar force; in which passages, by the vicious neglect of the rule, God and Christ have been separated into two persons, in our public version, contrary to the intention of the original writer, and the undoubted idiom of the language in which he wrote.*

"According to our own opinion, formed with the strictest attention to the evidence produced, this rule, as stated by Mr. Sharp, appeared perfectly clear, and the deductions from it no less than inevitable. We considered it as founded in truth and demonstrated with ability. But we see, with much additional satisfaction, the explicit testimony of so great a master of Greek literature as Mr. Burgess, stated in the second edition of the Remarks. His opinion was before implied in the act of publishing the Remarks, and was otherwise intimated in the first edition; but it is now, in an introductory letter to Mr. Sharp, expressed in the strongest terms.

'That you have happily and decisively applied your rule of construction to the correction of the common English version

---

* "The rule may be thus briefly and loosely expressed, though to be strictly accurate it will require, as Mr. Sharp has given it, more limitations. 'When two nouns descriptive of a person, and united by a conjunction, have only one article prefixed to both, they are both intended to describe the same person.' This rule is uniformly followed by all Greek writers."

of the New Testament, and to the *perfect establishment* of the great doctrine in question, the DIVINITY of CHRIST, no impartial reader, I think, can doubt, *who is at all acquainted with the original language of the New Testament.*'

"When it is considered that the writer who gives this testimony is Mr. Burgess, whose knowledge of the Greek language qualified him, very early in life, to produce a much improved edition of one of the acutest books we have on Greek literature, *Dawes' Miscellanea Critica*; and who, from that time to this, has distinguished himself by various works illustrative of the Greek language and the authors who have used it, the force and value of the decision may be duly estimated. Speaking farther of the rule in question, the same learned editor says to Mr. Sharp, 'I call the rule *yours*; for, though it was acknowledged and applied by Beza and others* to some of the texts alleged by you, yet never was it so prominently, because singly, or so effectually, as in your Remarks.' This testimony of Theodore Beza, an acknowledged scholar, and a translator of the whole New Testament, is particularly valuable; and, as it has not been given at length, in what has hitherto been published, we shall

---

* "Beza is not the only one among the biblical critics who has noticed this idiom; it has occasionally been urged by various writers. Abundant praise is due to Mr. Granville Sharp for bringing it forward in the distinct manner he has, and for illustrating it by so great a variety of apposite examples; but we must not, if we would be correct, consider it as his discovery even among the moderns. Wolfius says, 'Articulus τοῦ pæmittendus fuisset voci Σωτηρος (in Tit. 2:13) siquidem hic a μεγαλῳ Θεῳ distingui debuisset.' *In loco.* Drusius, on the same text, says, "Non solum Deus, fed eitam *Deus Magnus*, vocatur hic Christus' (in Crit. Sacro); where, though the rule is not mentioned, it is taken for granted as undeniable. Bishop Bull, Calovius, Vitringa, and Dr. Twells, are all referred to by Wolfius as supporting this sense, on the verse of Titus above-mentioned: and Erasmus, who speaks of that passage as ambiguous, had too much knowledge of Greek not to own, that the omission of the article had some force against that opinion. 'Quanquam *omissus articulus*, in libris Gæcis, facit *nonnihil* pro diveria sententâ. Μεγαλου Θεου και Σωτηρος, evidentius distinxisset personas fi dixisset, και του Σωτηρος,' *Rev.* "

here insert it. In commenting on the text, Tit. 2:13, επιφανειαν της δοξης του μεγαλου Θεου και Σωτηρος ἡμων Ιησου Χριστου, after speaking of the επιφανεια, which he rightly insists must belong to Christ, and which he translates *adventus,* he thus proceeds: 'Quod autem ad alterum attinet quum scriptum sit, ε. του μεγαλου Θεου και του Σωτηρος ἡμων I. X. non autem του μεγαλου Θεου και του Σωτνρος, dico non magis probabiliter ifta posse ad duas distinctas personas referri, quam illam locutionem ὁ Θεος και Πατηρ Ιησου Χριστου. Nam id certe postulat Græci sermonis usus, *quum unus tantum sit articulus, duobus istis,* nempe Θεου και Σωτηρος, Θεος και Πατηρ, *communis*: qumm præsertim, ut ante dixi, nunquam επιφανεια aut παρουσια nisi uni Filio tribuatur. Itaque sic concludo, Christum Jesum hic apertè Magnum Deum dici, qui et beata illa spes nostra metonymice vocatur. Illi igitur ut verè magno et æterno Deo, sit gloria et laus omnis, in sæcula sæculorum.' Here the rule, respecting the article, is distinctly laid down, as by Mr. Sharp, and the same conclusion, with equal distinctness, drawn.

"But the authority of Beza, or of any modern, was not sufficient for the ingenious writer of these Six Letters.* He thought of a higher appeal, to the Greek Fathers; as men who could not but be competent judges of their native language. 'If Mr. Sharp's rule be true,' said he, 'then will *their* interpretation of those texts be invariably in the same sense in which he understands them,' p. 3. To these judges, then, he appealed; and, by a most laborious examination of their works, has produced such an additional testimony, in behalf

---

* "This writer we learn, on inquiry, to be Mr. C. Wordsworth, of Trinity-college, Cambridge; who, though he modestly withheld his name at first, is not, we understand, anxious to be concealed."

of the rule, as cannot fail to astonish those who are most unwilling to be convinced. When we think of examining, for a few texts, the voluminous works of seventy Greek and near sixty Latin Fathers and other divines, besides theological collections of great magnitude, we think of a labor which resembles rather the indefatigable diligence of former times than the supineness of modern research. Yet such was the origin of the present volume," (the 6 letters,) "and such the industry and acuteness employed to furnish the materials.

"In the sequel to Mr. Sharp's remarks are nine examples of his first rule, eight of which are such as must, by their genuine application, introduce important alterations in the version, and become, only by being rightly translated, direct assertions of the Divinity of Christ.*   These eight examples, therefore, are made the subject of the present letters, in which they are regularly discussed in order, as to the manner in which they were read and understood by the ancient Fathers.[†] In making this examination, to the extent which we have already mentioned, the most important results were found, as might be expected, in the writings of the Greek Fathers: and, as we have stated the appeal to their accurate knowledge of their own language as the chief object of these letters, we shall, in our report upon them pay little attention to any other authorities.

* "The remaining example, which is the third in order, has no operation of that kind, and seems to be introduced chiefly for the sake of establishing the reading πνευματι Θεου, from the Alexandrian and other MSS in Philip. 3:3. See p. 31, 2d edit."

† "They are set down together at p. vi."

"1. The first of these eight examples adduced by Mr. Sharp* is Acts, 20:28; but, as this is not applicable unless του Κυριου και Θεου can be proved to be the genuine reading, which is very doubtful,[†] it is passed over in these letters. [‡] But the question concerning the right reading still remains open.

"2. The second example is Ephes. 5:5, ουκ εχει κληρονομιαν εν τη βασιλεια του Χριστου και Θεου, § rendered, in our common translation, 'hath any inheritance in the kingdom of Christ and of God;' but, according to an explanatory substitution, usual with our translators in other cases, 'of Christ, *even* of God;' meaning that it is one and the same person who is here called both Christ and God. The examination here taken up[¶] is, whether this text was so understood by the Greek Fathers, or in any other way. The conclusion is, as this author tells his correspondent, 'that no other interpretation than *yours*, (Mr. Sharp's) was ever heard in all the Greek churches.' The passages that most remarkably prove this (for we cannot be expected to cite them all, or to notice the incidental discussions**) are the following: 1. A passage in the fifth Homily of St. Chrysostom, on the incomprehensible nature of God, where this text is cited, with three other of the strongest scriptural

* "P. 27, second edit."

† "Bengelius notices this reading, but marks it with ε, one of his signs of disapprobation."

‡ "See Letter II. p.12."

§ "Sharp, p. 30."

¶ "Letter II. p. 12."

** "These are numerous, and the extreme candor and caution of the author appear in every instance."

declarations, to show that Christ is God. 2. A passage from Cyrill of Alexandria, who, after quoting this verse from the Ephesians, says, Ιδου παλιν Χριστον ονομασας ευθυς αυτον εισφερει και Θεον. 'Observe, again, that, having named Christ, he immediately adds, *that he is also God.*' In other parts of his works, the same Father cites this verse, as denominating our Saviour both Christ and God, Χριστον αυτον ωνομαζε και Θεον ούτω λεγων. 'He calls Christ himself God also, when he thus speaks,' namely, when he writes this verse. 3. The testimony of Theodoret is no less explicit, for he cites this verse, with that to Titus, (2:13) and others, expressly for the sake of proving that Christ is God; and in one of the passages inadvertently substitutes Χριστου του Θεου as perfectly equivalent to του Χριστου και Θεου. Having given these leading specimens, let us sum up the whole of what is done, respecting this verse, in the words of the letter-writer himself.

'We have referred to twenty-one Greek passages in which the words εν τη Βασιλεια του Χριστου και Θεου are quoted. Of these we consider twelve as determining nothing either way with respect to the meaning of those particular words; but then we observe, that it is not for the sake of those words their quotations are made. The remaining nine are, with one voice, clear testimonies for your (Mr. Sharp's) interpretation. That is, in fact, all the Greek authorities that do speak at all are on your side.' P. 36.

"Much discussion is also taken up in this letter concerning the comparative value of the Latin writers, and the weight of their testimony when they are contrary to the Greek: but this, which is managed with great judgement, we cannot repeat."

"3. On the next example,* (2 Thess. 2:12,) which is the subject of the third letter, it so happens that there are no decisive authorities. The verse appears not in the polemical writings of the Fathers, because it contains nothing decisive against the Arians,[†] with whom their chief controversies were carried on: and they who wrote continued commentaries saw no occasion to expatiate upon words which to them appeared perfectly clear. This example, therefore, does not long detain the writer of the letters, who is careful, however, to remark, that nothing appears against the proposed interpretation, and that several presumptions strongly favor it.

"4. In the fourth example, [‡] (1 Tim. 5:21,) we are again in part deserted by the reading of the text, the citations of the Fathers being made in general without the important word κυριου, [§] thus removing it from any application of the rule. It still, however, remains to be inquired which is the proper reading of the verse, by means of MSS and versions; a search which the present author does not fully undertake, (as being foreign to his immediate object,) but touches with great judgement. Mr. Sharp says that the word Χριστου is omitted

---

* "The third here, the fourth in Sharp, (p.34,) [Ed.- this edition p. 45] translated by him, 'according to the grace of Jesus Christ, our God and Lord.'"

† "Who allowed the Divinity of Christ, which this verse asserts, but conceived his Godhead to be of a secondary kind, against which it says nothing. Had it placed Christ before the Father it would have been often cited."

‡ "The fifth in Sharp, p.38 [Ed.- this edition p. 48]."

§ "Thus: ενοπιον [sic - ενωπιον] του Θεου και Ιησου Χριστου, which makes it no longer an example of Mr. Sharp's rule. The common reading is του Θεου και κυριου Ι. Χ. On looking back to our article on Mr. Sharp's book, (vol. xv. p. 71,) we perceive, that, in the hurry of a periodical press, we ourselves have omitted κυριου: a most material error. Also την before Χαριν, in the preceding text."

in the Alexandrian MS contrary to the authority of Wetstein and Griesbach, who assert it is κυριου. We have examined the MS itself, and find that Mr. S. is in this instance mistaken, and that κυριου is the word omitted, the text being ενωπιον ΤΟΥ ΘῩ ΚΑΙ ΧῩ ΙῩ, which are the undoubted abbreviations of Θεου και Χριστου Ιησου." [This error is corrected in the present edition, see note . . .] [Ed.- see note on pp. 48-49.]

"On this passage also occurs the only apparent contradiction of Mr. Sharp's rule which the whole research has produced, in three citations, namely, from Chrysostom, Œcumenius, and Theophylact, in which του Θεου και κυριου is retained, and yet the words are interpreted of two persons. As the only solution of this difficulty, Mr. Wordsworth suggests that the MSS of these writers had not κυριου, which, with respect to the two latter, appears probable. But here he does not quite retain his usual acuteness; for, Chrysostom (unless it be an error of the press in this book) must have had κυριου, as he has, peculiarly to himself, the additional word ἡμων subjoined. But it may fairly be conjectured that he read it και ΤΟΥ κυριου ἡμων, which, by inserting the article again, equally removes it from the influence of our rule. As a collateral proof (and a very strong one it is) that the inconsistency of construction, apparently found in these three passages, could not really belong to them, this author observes that similar phrases in the same three Greek Fathers,* and the very words ὁ Θεος και κυριος, in twenty-six citations from others, are

---

* "It is a very singular and curious proof of diligence that the author of these letters should be able to say (even with the modesty he observes in it) of four small words, ὁ Θεος και κυριος, that they occur together but once in the twelve huge folios of Chrysostom. The one passage in that writer is τον κοινον ἡμων Θεον και κυριον τον Χριστον. A very strong one in all respects. See p. 56."

uniformly referred to one person."

"5. The fifth example, * (2 Tim. 4:1,) which is nearly in the same words as the preceding, shares a very similar fate, being removed from the influence of the rule by the repetition of the article του Θεου και του κυριου. Mr. Sharp, however, alleges that του Θεου και κυριου is the reading of the Alexandrian MS. But the text of that MS gives, as in the former passage, ΤΟΥ ΘΥ ΚΑΙ ΧΥ ΙΥ, του Θεου και Χριστου Ιησου. [This error is also corrected in the present edition, see note . . .] [Ed.- see note, pp. 48-49.] It remains, therefore, to confirm the reading he supports by other authorities. [For which see note in 3d. edit. p. . . .] [Ed.- see notes, pp. 50-53].

"6. If we have had difficulties respecting the readings of some of these examples, we shall have none in that to which we are now arrived.[†] It is that in the Epistle of St. Paul to Titus, (2:13,) επιφανειαν της δοξης του μεγαλου Θεου και Σωτηρος ημων Ιησου Χριστου: a text of which the reading is uniform, and the interpretation of the Fathers exactly consistent with that at present under consideration. The text was urged by them, in general, against the Arians; not to prove that Christ is God, for that was granted by both parties, but to prove that his Godhead is not inferior to that of the Father, because the Apostle here calls him the "GREAT GOD." To this argument it was indispensably necessary that the passage should be understood according to Mr. Sharp's translation, 'the appearance of the glory of our GREAT GOD and SAVIOUR, JESUS CHRIST;' and not according to our public version, 'the great God, AND our Saviour Jesus Christ.'

* "Sharp's 6th, p.39."

† "Mr. Sharp's 7th Ex. p. 42. Of these letters the 5th, p.65."

"On this text the authorities are so decisive that we shall content ourselves with recounting their numbers instead of estimating their force. The Greek authorities are fifty-four in number, as cited in these Letters,* and extend from the second century to the twelfth, a period of nearly a thousand years. In this instance, also, the Latin fathers and divines bear the same testimony, with very few and inconsiderable exceptions, and are cited to this effect in about sixty instances. Even the heretics of the Latin church, till very late times, acknowledged the interpretation contended for by Mr. Sharp; and that adopted in our public version 'was never one thought of in any part of the Christian world, even when Arianism was triumphant over the Catholic faith. Surely,' adds the author of these Letters, and we heartily add with him, 'this fact might of itself suffice to overturn every notion of an ambiguity in the form of expression.' P. 95. The perfect establishment even of this one text, in the sense here ascribed to it, if that were all that could be done, ought to give the Socinian some apprehension, when he presumes to degrade to the rank of a mere man, him whom the Apostle Paul unequivocally styles 'the GREAT GOD.' We believe, indeed, with the author of the Letters, that even the leaders of the sect have had their secret compunctions on this subject.[†]

"7. Of the two remaining examples we must expect to find less illustration. The Catholic Epistles were less quoted, and less commented upon, than those of St. Paul; and even Chrysostom, voluminous as he is, deserts us when we come to the second Epistle of St. Peter. The seventh example[‡] is taken from that Epistle, 2 Pet. 1:1. Εν δικαιοσυνῃ του

---

* "And the author shows that he could have increased them."

† "See p. 66."

‡ "Sharp 8th, p. 44. Letter VI. p. 103."

Θεου ἡμων και Σωτηρος Ιησου Χριστου, that is, in the common version, 'through the righteousness of God* and our Saviour Jesus Christ:' in Mr. Sharp's rendering, 'through the righteousness of *our God and Saviour*, Jesus Christ.' The authorities of the Fathers, both Greek and Latin, are here neutral; but it is something of importance to our inquiry, (which is noted by Mr. Sharp,) that Wickliff, Coverdale, Matthews, Cranmer, the Geneva and Rhemish Bibles, Doddridge, Scattergood, Wesley, and Purver, all translate the words according to his rule.

"8. We come now to the last of these examples, Jude, ver. 4, τον μονον δεσποτην, Θεον, και κυριον ἡμων, Ιησουν Χριστον, αρνουμενοι, † 'denying our only Master, God, and Lord, Jesus Christ.' Here is some difficulty in the reading, Θεον being wanting in many MSS. The chief testimony adduced is from some scholia of the 11th century, published by Professor Matthæi, which conclude ὁτι ἑις εστιν ὁ παλαιας και νεας διαθηκης Θεος και κυριος, Ιησους Χριστος. 'That there is one Jesus Christ, the God and Lord of the Old and New Testaments.'

"We should here finish, but that the author of these Letters has suggested a new passage as belonging to the same interpretation, though not to the same rule. ‡

* "Erroneously printed, in Mr. Sharp's remarks, 'of *our* God.' P. 45, 2d edit." (Corrected 3d edit. p. 51.) [*sic* - p. 52.] [Ed.- see p. 56 of this edition.]

† "Sharp's Ex. 9, p. 46. Letters, p. 108."

‡ "See also Rev. 19:17, if the true reading there should turn out to be δειπνον του μεγαλου Θεου, instead of δ. το μεγα του Θ. See p. 66."

This is James, 1:1, Ιακωβος Θεου και κυριου Ιησου Χριστου δουλος, where, though the article is not prefixed to Θεου, it is thought probable, and by some proofs much confirmed, that the Apostle meant to style himself, 'a servant of our God and Lord, Jesus Christ.' The author concludes his collection by various passages, from twenty different Greek writers, exemplifying the alleged use of the article, and many of them strongly declaring the Godhead of Christ.

"Thus have we completely shown the substance of the information contained in these Letters.   It is extremely important; and, though the candor of the letter-writer prevents him from attempting to take advantage of any dubious text or readings, the whole mass of evidence which he has collected is abundantly strong and valuable.   The work is rendered of additional value by supplemental tables of the Greek and Latin Fathers, placed in chronological order, with some account of their extent and of the editions used by the author. We cannot conclude without recommending to every diligent student in divinity to read both this book and that of Mr. Sharp, to confirm themselves in that doctrine of which the primitive church never entertained a doubt,* the 'DIVINITY of our BLESSED SAVIOUR.'   Nor shall we attempt to conceal, that we view with great pleasure these rational endeavors to support a doctrine so fundamental to our religion."

---

* "Notwithstanding the daring assertions that have, in modern times, been made to the contrary."

———《《》》———

Review of G. Sharp's Remarks on the uses of the Definite Article, and on the Six Letters to G. Sharp, in the CHRISTIAN OBSERVER for July, 1802. No. VII. vol. i. p. 438, art. xxvii.

After reciting the first rule proposed by G. Sharp, the learned reviewer remarks,

"This rule is valuable, not merely in a philological view, but because it enables us to correct the translation of several passages in the New Testament, which, properly understood, afford 'many striking proofs concerning the godhead of our Lord and Saviour Jesus Christ.' Under this idea we are referred to the following passages. Acts 20:28. Eph. 5:5. 2 Thess. 1:12. 1 Tim. 5:21. 2 Tim. 4:1. Titus 2:13. 2 Pet. 1:1. Jude 4.

"The Six Letters addressed to G. Sharp, Esq. (which we have heard attributed to the Rev. C. Wordsworth, M.A. and Fellow of Trinity College, Cambridge) may be considered as an important supplement to his work. It seems reasonable to suppose, that, if Mr. Sharp's rule be true, the ancient interpretations of any particular example by the Greek fathers must tend to confirm it. The object of this work, therefore, is to examine, by actual reference, what were the opinions of the early Greek writers upon those eight texts which are mentioned above. In the course of this learned and most laborious investigation, the author not only proves, by a great variety of quotations, in what sense the fathers understood these passages, but shows, farther, at what time and amongst what writers the interpretation began to be ambiguous. To any one at all conversant with the Latin and Greek languages it cannot be a matter of astonishment, if, for want of the definite article, an ambiguity frequently occurs in the Latin translation of a Greek sentence, where there is no difficulty whatever in the original. And to this source the author traces the uncertainty which has so long existed with respect to the true meaning of the texts cited by Mr. Sharp. Few of the Latin fathers were conversant with Greek; they quoted in general from their own translations, and therefore generally adopted that sense which, to a mere Latin reader, would appear the most obvious. If, then, the Greek and Latin writers seem to differ with respect to the meaning of a Greek passage, the question to us becomes this: 'Shall we take the explanation of a Greek passage from Greeks or prefer from Latin writers, not the explanation of the Greek, but of a *translation* of it into their language; which translation, though capable of *both* meanings, and so originally not a false translation, would much more naturally lead men to that sense which is contradictory to the common Grecian idiom and the uniform voice of Grecian interpreters?' p. 38. As our limits will not allow us to follow this author through his numerous and truly valuable quotations, let it suffice to state the general result. It appears, then, that where there is no reason to suppose a different reading obtained from that adopted by Mr. Sharp, the Greek writers are decisive in support of his interpretation; the contradictions and ambiguities rest with the Latin writers. In the second, fifth, and sixth, Letters, the quotations are numerous and highly satisfactory: they prove, incontestably, that words arranged according to the rule never did, from the times of the Apostles, bear any other sense than that assigned by Mr. Sharp during the period while the Greek was a native language. This remark is not to be understood as applicable merely to the verses in question, but as extending to this mode of expression wherever it is used. In proof of this assertion, a considerable number of passages is here produced from the earliest fathers down to the thirteenth century: and the author adds, 'I have observed more (I am persuaded) than a thousand instances of the form "Ο Χριστος και Θεος,"

(Ephes. 5:5.); some hundreds of instances of the "Ο μεγας Θεος και Σωτηρ," (Tit. 2:13.); and not fewer than several thousands of the form "Ο Θεος και Σωτηρ," (2 Pet. 1:1.); while in no single case have I seen (where the sense could be determined) any one of them used, but only of one person.' p. 132. Nay, the Arians themselves, it should seem, even at a time when their heresy was triumphant, acknowledged this construction, in admitting that Christ is styled, by St. Paul, the great God. The words of Maximin, the Arian Bishop, as cited in this work, (p. 95,) are very remarkable:

"A nobis unus colitur Deus, innatus, infectus, invisibilis, qui ad humana contagia, et ad humanam carnem non descendit. Est autem et filius secundum apostolum, non pusillus, sed magnus Deus. Sicut ait beatus Paulus:" "Expectantes beatam spem et adventum gloriæ magni Dei et Salvatoris nostri Jesu Christi, etc."

They did not deny that Christ is here called the great God, but contended that the Father was greater."

Towards the close of his work the author suggests some philological remarks, which well merit attention.

We cannot dismiss this article without offering a few remarks upon the subject which this work is meant to examine. The rule laid down by Mr. Sharp was originally proposed by Beza: his words relating to the passage in Titus are the following: *"Quod autem ad alterum attinet, quum scriptum sit,"* "επιφανειαν του μεγαλου Θεου και Σωτηρος ήμων Ιησου Χριστου, *non autem*, του μεγαλου Θεου και ΤΟΥ Σωτηρος, etc. *dico non magis probabiliter ista posse ad duas distinctas personas referri, quam illam locutionem,* "ὁ Θεος και πατηρ Ιησου Χριστου." *Nam id certe postulat Græci sermonis usus, quum unus tantum sit*

articulus, duobus istis nempe, "Θεου και Σωτηρος" *et*
"Θεος και πατηρ" *communis.*" The rule, however, not
being laid down with sufficient accuracy, and a due regard to
the exceptions of a proper name and a plural number,
Erasmus and Grotius paid little regard to it. Since that
period it has often been asserted or denied, according to the
preconceived opinions of different writers; it has been
generally admitted that it *might* be true, but contended on the
other hand that it might also be false. Mr. Sharp was the
first who laid down the rule with clearness and precision,
declaring the words thus arranged *must* bear this
construction, and *can* bear no other. The public have now
been for some years in possession of it; and we believe it has
never yet been controverted by any man. The rule must have
been known to his learned Editor, Mr. Burgess, some time
before; yet it seems a fair presumption that no exceptions
have come under his notice, for he has lately published a
second edition of the same pamphlet.* The information
contained in the Six Letters is calculated to give the strongest
support and most ample conformation to the rule. In this
view, therefore, we consider this work as of very great
importance; it enlists into the service of the catholic faith
several texts which have been frequently claimed by Arians
and Socinians, as exclusively in their favor; thus depriving
heresy of one of its greatest strong-holds, and affording
another proof of the doctrine of the Trinity, which it will not
be easy to elude.

* "We have heard the question advanced, 'Does Mr. Sharp's first rule obtain in
the Septuagint and classical Greek writers?' This mode of expression does not
often occur in the LXX.; but where it does occur, we believe, all the instances are
in favor of this construction; if we mistake not, the first example which can be
produced is in Levit. 21:10. In the writings of the Greek classics we have noticed
hundreds of instances, and have not yet seen one which makes against the rule.
Take an example or two: Οι δε, ατε ου δωροδοκοι οντες, καταφρονουσιν
απαντων τουτων, ως φησι Ο Θεος ΚΑΙ Θεων προφητης (viz. Homer:)
Plato's 2d Alcibiad. Και γαρ τοι πεμψαρ Ιππονικον Ο συμμαχορ ΚΑΙ
φιλος αυτοις Φιλιππος. (Demosth. κατα Φιλιππον, Λογος γ.)"

"Feeling, as we do, the fullest conviction, that a body of evidence is here brought forward which the adversaries of our faith can neither gainsay nor resist, we challenge them to examination of it: if Mr. Sharp's rule be false, let them prove it by an appeal to the Greek Testament; if the quotations in these Letters can bear any other construction than that which the Author gives them, let another interpretation be produced. Till this shall be done, and we are persuaded it never can be done, we do most earnestly recommend this learned work to all those who are able to appreciate the value of such evidence, and are desirous to 'contend earnestly for that faith which was once delivered to the saints.'

"For the sake of the mere English reader, we subjoin a translation of the passages mentioned by Mr. Sharp, according to his rule, and the interpretations of the Greek fathers: we omit the first and fifth, because the reading in our common editions of the Greek Testament is different from that adopted by Mr. Sharp.

Ephes. 5:5. 'For this ye know, that no whoremonger, etc. hath any inheritance in the kingdom of him who is Christ and God.'

2 Thes. 1:12. —'according to the grace of Jesus Christ, our God and Lord.'

1 Tim. 5:21. 'I charge thee, before Jesus Christ, the God and Lord,' etc.

Titus 2:13. 'Looking for that blessed hope, and the glorious appearing of Jesus Christ, the great God and our Saviour.'

2 Pet. 1:1. 'Through the righteousness of Jesus Christ, our God and Saviour.'

Jude 4. 'And our only Master, God, and Lord, Jesus Christ.' "

The reader is requested to examine also a very learned, sensible, and candid, review, in answer to Mr. Blunt's *Six more Letters to G.S.* on the same subject, in the *Christian Observer* for June, 1803, No. vi. p. 363.

CHRISTIAN GUARDIAN.

Extract from the CHRISTIAN GUARDIAN, for December, 1802, Number XII. p. 348.

"Remarks on the Uses of the Definite Article in the Greek Text of the New Testament, etc., by Granville Sharp, Esq.: to which is added an Appendix, containing, 1. A table of evidences of Christ's divinity, by Dr. Whitby; 2. A plain argument from the Gospel History of the divinity of Christ, by the editor, the Rev. T. Burgess, Prebendary of Durham. pp. 80 ff.

"The new species of argument which is here so happily adduced, and addressed to the learned world, in support of the doctrine of our Saviours' divinity, not only merits the grateful attention of its friends, but imperiously demands the diligent scrutiny of its most inveterate enemies. It approaches so nearly to mathematical demonstration that we conceive it to be absolutely incapable of confutation. The school of Socinus was never attacked with a more formidable weapon; and it is with pleasure we see this treatise particularly recommended, in the preface, to Mr. Wakefield's most deliberate consideration.

"It would be impossible for us, in our analysis, to do justice to the elaborate work before us, without transcribing a very considerable portion of its invaluable contents. We will, however, communicate so much as may enable the judicious part of our readers to form a true estimate of the force of the arguments employed, and excite in them a powerful desire of becoming acquainted with it at full length.

After reciting the rules and referring to the examples, the learned Reviewer makes the following observation, in p. 350, on the Appendix:

"Mr. Burgess's plain argument, from the Gospel history, for the divinity of Christ, is drawn up by the way of question and answer, and forms a kind of catechism on the subject, comprised within the space of fourteen pages. The argument is arranged with such judicious simplicity and perspicuity, as must carry irresistible conviction to the understanding of every man who possesses in his heart a sincere love of truth; and who is not influenced by passion or prejudice to prefer darkness before light."

ORTHODOX CHURCHMAN.

Review of G. Sharp's Remarks on the uses of the Definite Article, and on the Six Letters to G. Sharp, in the ORTHODOX CHURCHMAN'S MAGAZINE AND REVIEW for February, 1803. No. IL. vol. iv. p. 105.

"These two works we introduce together, to the notice of our readers, on account of their intimate connection with each other.

"The principal object of the former is, to deduce from the New Testament an important rule with regard to the structure of the Greek language; and afterwards to apply that rule to the correction of the translation of several passages in our established English version of the Scriptures, which passages will be found, when rendered according to Mr.

Sharp's ideas, to contain the most express testimonies to the divinity of our Saviour. The rule in question is briefly this: 'whenever two personal nouns come together, (excepting proper names,) which are connected by the particle και, and to the former of which any case of the definite article is prefixed, both those nouns are invariably to be understood of the same person.' A large collection of passages from the New Testament is here exhibited, to afford sufficient and satisfactory instances of the rule thus laid down. After which Mr. S. points out certain other texts, which, containing in the original precisely the same construction, ought, he affirms, (and we apprehend with the fullest justice,) to be so translated as to convey to the English reader that they are to be understood (according to the rule) of the same person. The text referred to by Mr. S. and which bring with them, according to his system, the very important doctrinal conclusions which we have briefly mentioned, are the following: Acts, 20:28. (if we follow the reading, του Κυριου και Θεου.) Ephes. 5:5. 2 Thes. 1:12. 1 Tim. 5:21. 2 Tim. 4:1 (if we read του Θεου και Κυριου.) Titus 2:13. 2 Peter 1:1. Jude 4. All of which are, therefore, to be rendered severally in these significations:

(1.) The Church of him who is Lord and God.

(2.) In the kingdom of Christ, our God.

(3.) According to the grace of Jesus Christ, our God and Lord.

(4.) Before Jesus Christ, our God and Lord.

(5.) Before Jesus Christ, our God and Lord.

(6.) The glorious appearing of Jesus Christ, our great God and Saviour.

(7.) Of our God and Saviour, Jesus Christ.

(8.) Our only master Jesus Christ, both God and Lord.

"The importance of this rule, especially on account of the very striking conclusions to which it thus leads us, will we trust sufficiently recommend it to the strictest investigation and scrutiny of the learned world. For ourselves we freely declare, that, having given the subject a considerable portion of our attention, we find, daily, fresh instances and exemplifications of the rule, and as yet have met with nothing which in any respect tends to impeach its certainty and universality. For, it must be observed, that, though Mr. S. has drawn all his examples from the New Testament, yet the rule itself he has expressed in general terms; and the application of it, therefore, is by no means to be confined to the books of the New Testament. His reasons for not himself applying it to classical and other Greek writers were, probably, that in so doing he must have greatly extended his work, without any equivalent advantage: whilst, by asserting the rule in general terms, he has boldly submitted it to the scrutiny of all readers of all kinds of Greek books, and has thereby put the public, we apprehend, into a much surer road of attaining a speedy and certain knowledge of its extent and truth, than he could have done by a long, tedious, and after all very unsatisfactory, accumulation of passages from all the wide extent of Grecian literature. Let the thousands of readers of Greek produce a few instances* to contradict the rule, and then will be the proper time to consider whether or no it must be given up for ever.

---

* "As we consider the subject which we are now upon as of the very first magnitude, we shall be happy if any of our readers will favor us with communications (should they meet with them) to such effect. And we should be equally glad to insert any additional citations in the Fathers which may have escaped the vigilance of the writer of the "Six Letters;" or any particulars which may tend to supply the deficiencies, or remove the difficulties, still remaining in the investigation."

"The conclusions, however, which Mr. Sharp has drawn with regard to the interpretation of those texts of the New Testament above referred to, seem, in general, to be secured within a second wall by the interesting, and we will say *surprising*, result of the investigation of the laborious author of the "Six Letters." The general object of which work is, to arrive at those same conclusions by another road; to establish the same truths by a second perfectly distinct train of reasoning. 'It occurred to me,' (says this author,) 'that I should probably find some, at least, of those texts, the vulgar interpretation of which you have called in question, cited and explained by the ancient Fathers; not, indeed, as instances of any particular rule, but expounded by them *naturally*, as men would understand any other form of expression in their native language,' If these interpretations, thus discovered, should differ from Mr. Sharp's interpretation, it would seem to follow that his rule could not be true: if they accorded with his, it would then seem that those conclusions must now for a *second* reason be admitted; and the vulgar interpretation ought of course to be reformed according to the standard of the primitive authorities. This inference, however, would be still farther secured, if we should discover, from our investigation, that those heretics who were most pressed with these passages of Scripture, while Greek was understood as a living language, never devised so ready an expedient of eluding their force as modern ages have perpetually had recourse to, viz. a pretended ambiguity in the form of expression in the original; — and if it should still farther appear, in other instances, that the orthodox never betook themselves to this alleged ambiguity, even in those cases where it may be shown they must, from their principles, naturally have been inclined to do so.

"Upon this simple and unobjectionable ground work these letters are founded. The remaining five, after the first, are principally occupied in laying before us, in a chronological order, the result of the author's inquiries on each particular text; and they present an example of well-directed patience and perseverance which has seldom been surpassed. Almost all the vast remains of the Greek Fathers, and a great part of the Latin, appear to have been closely examined; and, what is scarcely of less importance, the labor seems to have been carried on, as the work is written, in a sober, cautious, and candid, temper. We cannot give a more correct general description of the work than by saying that it contains, as far as materials could be found, a history of the interpretation of the texts in question, from the earliest times nearly to the age of the reformation. With regard to more modern translators and commentators, Mr. S. has given sufficient information in the latter part of his "Remarks." It is an important advantage of this history that we learn from it not only what is true, but we discover also the origin and progress of the false modern interpretation. The origin is undoubtedly to be traced to the imperfection of the Latin language; and the progress was accelerated and increased by the great number of Latin commentators, by the greater familiarity of our early interpreters with those writers; perhaps, also, by the inclination to heterodoxy in Erasmus and others; and not a little, probably, by the reserve and timorousness of certain orthodox writers, forbearing and fearing to assert the true interpretation, not because they themselves did not hold it, but out of a love of peace, and because they knew it was denied or dislike by others.

"Having mentioned Mr. Sharp's conclusions, it seems but right that we should point out how far they appear to be established, or otherwise, by this second investigation.

"In the first, fourth, and fifth, instances, the readings in the Fathers do not correspond with Mr. Sharps' readings, and therefore the interpretation *is, as it ought to be*, different. In the second it is proved, to our satisfaction, 'that no other interpretation than Mr. Sharp's was ever heard in all the Greek churches;' and, farther, (what may seem strange to those who come to the consideration of the subject only with modern ideas,) that, *if* they *could*, the Greeks *would*, (as the Latins *did*) have interpreted it otherwise. On the third example the quotations are less numerous and less satisfactory; sufficient, however, when combined with a series of other quotations, given in the fourth letter, to corroborate the general conclusion. The sixth instance, by far the most important of all, is confirmed by a profusion of evidence. The seventh and eighth have again little *direct* evidence; but what we have affirmed of the third is, we apprehend, true of them also.

"In the last letter a long series of instances is given tending to show, that, from the very times of the Apostles, the identical forms of expression used in these texts of St. Paul, etc., were applied *perpetually* and *invariably* in the sense which is agreeable to Mr. Sharps' rule; and hence proving sufficiently in what sense even those writers who have not quoted them did understand, and would have explained and interpreted, the passages in question.

"In this last letter, also, authorities are given which render it probable that the text of St. James, 1:1, is to be added to those in which our Saviour Christ is called God.

"Having thus given a view of the contents of these publications, we shall conclude with earnestly recommending them to the notice of the public; and especially to those who have imbibed an inclination to Socinianism, to which system a blow seems to be here given which must spread a sickness through the whole frame. And, though far from being prejudiced in favor of novelties in divinity, we cannot but add that these works are, in our estimation, calculated to produce the most remarkable change which has long been witnessed in the theological world; and as constituting together, though of small size, the most important defense of Christian doctrine which this age, by no means deficient in such, has produced. For, what is here done (if *any* *thing* be done) will have the remarkable distinction of being done *once for all*, and must be not of a confined and temporary, but a universal and perpetual, efficacy."

In a Letter to the Editors of this Review, the reader will find a very just and sensible censure of Mr. Blunt's "Six More Letters to G.S." The said letter is published in the ORTHODOX CHURCHMAN's MAGAZINE for June, 1803, No. xxx; being the sixth number of vol. iv. p. 347.

INDEX

To the Texts cited in the preceding Work & Extracts
(Listed Alphanumerically)

1 Corinthians
    1:24 30
    4:5 70
    8:6 21
    10:9 69
    15:24 . . . . 13, 41
    15:3 71
1 John
    2:2 71
    3:8 72
    5:20 . . . . 69, 79
1 Peter
    1:3 41
    2:17 20
    4:11 28
    5:4 17
1 Thessalonians
    1:3 13,41
    3:6 28
    3:11 . . . . 12, 41
    3:13 . . . . 13, 41
    4:3,6 66
1 Timothy
    1:1 . . . . 21, 37
    1:2 22
    3:16 . . . . 69, 79
    5:21 . . . . . . 4, 48, 50, 51, 53, 54, 90, 96, 100, 103
    6:14 37

2 Corinthians
    1:2 24
    1:3 . . . . 3, 4, 9
    1:13 41
    4:3 18
    11:31 . . . . 9, 41
2 John
    1:3 22
2 Kings
    17:35,36 20
2 Peter
    1:1 . . . . 3, 4, 34, 35, 56, 93, 96, 98, 100, 103
    2:20 10
    3:2 10
    3:18 10
2 Thessalonians
    1:12 . . . . 45, 55, 84, 96, 100, 103
    2:8 37
    2:12 90
    2:16 13
    3:13 41
    3:16 70
    4:12 . . . . 3, 4
2 Timothy
    1:2 22
    1:5 27
    1:10 37
    4:1 . . . . 37, 50, 54, 55, 92, 96, 103
    4:8 37
Acts
    1:6 78
    2:36 30
    4:12 72
    7:59 70
    9:14 70
    20:28 . . . . 39, 88, 96, 103

Colossians
1:3 . . . . 13, 41
1:12 13
1:16 . . . . 21, 70
1:17 . . . . 21, 70, 79
1:19 . . . . 65, 70
1:27 37
2:2 . . . . 11, 18, 41
2:2,3 27
2:9 . . . . 14, 65, 70, 79
3:17 . . . . 13, 41
3:24 70
Daniel
7:14 76
Ephesians
1:2 24
1:3 41
4:31 23
4:6 25
4:6,20 41
5:5 . . . . 3, 4, 42, 88, 96, 97, 100, 103
5:20 13
5:20,21 20
6:21 9
6:23 24
Ezekiel
37:24 17
Galatians
1:3 24
1:4 . . . . 13, 41
Hebrews
1:2 . . . . 21, 70
1:3 . . . . 70, 79
1:6 70
1:8 69

1:10 70
3:1 10
3:4 69
9:12 71
9:22 73
13:20 16

Isaiah
7:14 . . . . 74, 76
40:9,10,11 17

James
1:1 . . . . 23, 30, 95, 107
1:27 . . . . 3, 4, 13, 41
3:9 . . . . 13, 41

Jeremiah
23:6 76

John
1:1 . . . . 69, 70, 73, 79
1:2 69
1:3 . . . . 21, 69, 70, 79
1:14 . . . . 64, 79
1:17 25
1:18 . . . . 64, 73
1:29 15
2:19 70
2:22 26
2:25 70
3:13 73
3:16,18 64
3:35 75
4:23 44
4:24 45
4:42 15
5:18 75
5:19 75
5:21,22,23 69
5:22 75

5:23 . . . . 15, 65, 70
6:27 16
6:33, ... 73
6:62 73
7:17 66
8:58 69
10:14 17
10:18 70
10:27 17
10:30 . . . . 69, 75
10:33 75
11:43,44 26
12:41 69
16:14,15 69
17:17 72
17:24 73
17:5 . . . . 65, 73, 75
17:5. 73
18:5 69
20:27,28 29
20:28 . . . . 29, 69, 79
20:31 16
21:17 70
Jude
1:4 . . . . 3, 4, 57, 65, 94, 96, 100, 103
Leviticus
21:10 99
Luke
1:43 69
1:47 14
2:26 15
24:21 78
Mark
3:11 76
13:13 72
14:61,62 77

Matthew
    1:22,23 74
    1:23 79
    2:1 74
    2:5,6 74
    4:10 70
    12:22 9
    12:34 62
    16:23 78
    23:33 62
    26:41 72
Philemon
    :3 24
Philippians
    2:6 70
    2:6,7,8 73
    3:21 70
    3:3 . . . . 43, 87
    4:20 . . . . 11, 41
Psalm
    23:1 17
Psalms
    95:30 17
    95th 17
Revelation
    1:6 13
    1:8 32
    1:13 31
    1:17,18 30
    2:8 31
    16:15 11
    19:17 94
    20:2 33
    22:13 32

Romans

2:19,20 19
8:9 . . . . 44, 72
9:5 . . . . 69, 79
10:12 69
10:13 . . . . 69, 70
14:12 69
15:6 . . . . 13, 40

Titus

1:1 21
1:4 22
2:13 . . . . 3, 4, 35, 37, 55, 65, 69, 84-86, 89,
92, 96, 98, 100, 103
2:14 72